WE THE VOTERS

WE THE VOTERS

*The Constitutional Choices
That Shape America's Elections*

Lori A. Ringhand

STANFORD UNIVERSITY PRESS
Stanford, California

Stanford University Press
Stanford, California

Library of Congress Cataloging-in-Publication Data
Names: Ringhand, Lori A., author.
Title: We the voters : the constitutional choices that shape America's elections
    / Lori A. Ringhand.
Description: Stanford, California : Stanford University Press, 2026. |
    Includes index.
Identifiers: LCCN 2025022112 (print) | LCCN 2025022113 (ebook) |
    ISBN 9781503645486 (ebook) | ISBN 9781503645479 (cloth)
Subjects: LCSH: Election law—United States. | Constitutional law—United
    States.
Classification: LCC KF4886 (ebook) | LCC KF4886 .R56 2026 (print) |
    DDC 342.73/07 23/eng/20250—dc08
LC record available at https://lccn.loc.gov/2025022112

Cover design: Jan Šabach

The authorized representative in the EU for product safety and compliance is:
Mare Nostrum Group B.V. | Mauritskade 21D | 1091 GC Amsterdam | The
Netherlands | Email address: gpsr@mare-nostrum.co.uk | KVK chamber of
commerce number: 96249943

CONTENTS

PREFACE

If America is to remain committed to elections as a peaceful way to transfer political power, we need to do a better job of understanding how our democracy works, and why. Fortunately, many of us seem eager to do just that. Americans are brimming with questions about the Electoral College; the relative power of local, state, and federal officials in making rules about how we vote; the role of the Supreme Court and state legislatures in resolving election disputes; and a host of other election-related matters many Americans rarely had reason to think about before. There is a real hunger to move beyond the inflammatory rhetoric and self-interested rabble-rousing to try to understand why our elections work the way we do, and how we might be able to make them better.

This book is my effort to shed light on these questions, by going back to our foundational documents and explaining how the choices our founders made—or in some cases failed to make—continue to structure our system of self-government. In straightforward and accessible language, it explores the choices, cases, and compromises governing some of the most bedeviling issues that arise in election law: things like who "the people" are, how they should be represented in our institutions of government, who makes the rules governing our elections, and how those rules might be changed.

As we will see, our country has grappled with questions like this before. Since the founding, Americans repeatedly have evaluated whether their democracy is working. They also, when necessary, have changed it. As we will see, those changes take many forms but they all have come from us, the American people. Which is exactly as it should be, because our democracy is just that: ours. And how it works is up to us.

ACKNOWLEDGMENTS

This book would not have been possible without the help and support of many people. I received invaluable feedback from Dan Coenen, Paige Cole, Jacob Eisler, Atiba Ellis, Edward Foley, Anthony Gaughan, Mark Graber, Sanford Levinson, Justin Levitt, Dan Lorentz, Joseph Miller, Michael Morley, Derek Muller, and Logan Sawyer. I also am grateful for comments from several anonymous reviewers, the participants at the University of Wisconsin "Constitutional Law Schmooze," the Florida State College of Law's First Annual Program on Election Law, and the University of Wisconsin Law Review (which published an earlier piece addressing some of the issues raised in Chapter 4). I also am indebted to Marcela Maxfield and the team at the Stanford University Press for seeing the potential in this book and shepherding it through the publication process.

Destiny Burch, Madeleine Hoss, Anderson Scott, and Andrew Wilson provided important and tireless research support. Jessica Atkinson helped in innumerable ways, while University of Georgia law librarians Wendy Moore, Savanna Nolan, and Amy Taylor brought attention to detail, excellent book recommendations, and general good cheer to the entire project. I also was extraordinary lucky to have early support from the Stanton Foundation enabling me to prepare the undergraduate course that germinated this book and providing the research time to see it to fruition.

Finally, I want to thank the students who over the years have enrolled in that undergraduate course. Their endless enthusiasm, intellectual curiosity, and ceaseless yearning to know more and do better has been an enduring and priceless gift. With pride and gratitude, I dedicate this book to them.

Opinions and errors are of course my own.

WE THE VOTERS

Introduction

Democracy is not a state. It is an act, and each generation
must do its part . . .

— CONGRESSMAN JOHN LEWIS, 2020[1]

When you go to the polls to cast your ballot in presidential, congressional, state, and local elections, you are participating in a long tradition of democratic self-governance. From the revolutionaries of 1776, to the freedmen who risked their lives to vote after the Civil War, to those fighting for voting rights today, Americans have understood that voting is the bedrock of our democracy. But how democracy in America actually works has never been a simple or straightforward proposition. Questions about who gets to vote, how those votes are translated into political representation, and who makes the rules governing it all have divided Americans since the nation's founding. The story of American democracy, in other words, is the story of fighting over what democracy in America should be.

Those fights have at times been fierce. In 1776, establishing the right to govern ourselves required yanking the reins of power from the hands of a king. Our first effort at exercising that right, under the Articles of Confederation, was a flop and had to be replaced after just more than a decade. Expanding the right to include more people took a civil war, decades of activism, and multiple constitutional amendments. From disputes over how to divide political power under the original Constitution, through the voting rights movements of the twentieth century, to the heated battles of today about how to protect free and fair elections, Americans have disagreed, often sharply, about how our system of self-government should work.

As we will see, our founding documents give us a framework to debate these issues, but they rarely fully resolve certain recurring questions lurking just beneath their surface. Instead, each generation settles those questions contingently, through argument, legislation, constitutional amendment, and litigation. The choices those prior generations faced, the compromises they made, and the court cases interpreting their choices and compromises, have fundamentally shaped our system of self-government. Examining how these past decisions both empower and shape the choices we face today will enables us to better navigate questions about what the rules of our democracy are, and why.

In the coming chapters, we'll see how conflicts about how to best govern ourselves tend to revolve around the same set of basic questions. Who are "the people" entitled to participate in self-government? How should those people be represented in our institutions of government? And who gets to decide what the rules governing it all will be? Today, these questions undergird debates over things like whom to count when dividing up legislative districts, how we should elect our president, and whether it should be easier or harder for people to vote. But for prior generations the same questions arose in disputes over the distribution of power in the new federal government, how to count enslaved people for purposes of political representation, and whether things like literacy tests should be used to restrict access to the ballot. The goal of this book is to help us understand those past choices and how they continue to shape how democracy in America works today.

Chapter 1 begins our exploration of these issues by asking just what, exactly, our system of American self-government is. It does so by addressing what has become a common question in American politics: Is America a democracy or a republic? The chapter explores what those terms meant in revolutionary America and concludes, unsurprisingly, that we are both, and more: We are a democratic, representative, federalist, and constitutional republic. The chapter looks at the decision in 1776 to declare independence from the British, and the drafting eleven years later of the original Constitution. The Declaration of Independence shows that our country's commitment to self-government, while imperfectly realized, has been part of our national fiber from the very start. The 1787 Constitution shows how the authors of that document operationalized representative government in a new way, by channeling the sovereignty of the people through competing institutions, each representing and accountable to different people in different ways. Together, these documents create the foundation on which America's system of self-government is built.

After this discussion of our basic institutions of government, Chapter 2 turns to debates at the Constitutional Convention, held in Philadelphia in 1787, over how representation, and therefore political power, within those institutions would be divided among the people of the new nation. Specifically, this chapter looks at the framers' choices about how to structure the U.S. Senate and the House of Representatives and how those choices shape current debates about representation, majority rule, and legislative districting.

Chapter 3 focuses on the presidency. It explores the reasons underlying the unusual system we know as the Electoral College (a term that does not appear in the Constitution itself) and why the original design of that system was almost immediately abandoned. It goes on to look at how the Electoral College has contributed to heated disputes over recent presidential elections and discusses efforts throughout our history to change or clarify the process. It ends by asking whether a cobbled-together system designed by exhausted men in 1787 is really the best way for a large, diverse, and modern nation to elect its chief executive officer and discusses alternative systems we could consider adopting instead.

Chapter 4 explores the critical question of who gets to decide what the rules governing our elections are. This chapter explains how and why the Constitution splits responsibility for making election rules between the federal government and the state governments and how those entities have used their respective powers to create the complex systems governing how we vote. It also explains how two relatively obscure constitutional provisions underlie disputes today over things like preventing noncitizen voting, limiting partisan gerrymandering, and using state laws to constrain the power of state legislatures when they make rules regulating federal elections. The chapter ends by surveying the various rules and regulations in place across the country that help keep our elections safe and secure.

Chapter 5 is a more in-depth examination of how the definition of "we the people" has changed over time, specifically in relation to the long fight of Black Americans to participate and be represented in our system of government as full and equal citizens. It begins by looking at the Reconstruction Amendments, enacted after the Civil War, which for the first time enshrined in the federal Constitution a more inclusive definition of "the people" and gave the federal government the power to protect the rights of more Americans, including our right to participate as equals in our elections. It goes on to discuss how Congress has used its power under the Reconstruction Amendments to ensure that racial minorities have an equal opportunity to elect representatives of their choice to America's legislative bodies and how that power has been repeatedly contested and often constrained by the U.S. Supreme Court.

Chapter 6 turns to today's disputes about how to balance the right to vote with the need to protect the integrity of our elections. In the name of election security, states across the country have enacted laws making it more difficult for more people to cast their ballots. This chapter explores how the Constitution, specifically the Equal Protection Clause of the Fourteenth Amendment, does (and does not) limit the power of states and Congress to burden the right to vote through these types of laws. The book then concludes by discussing how the past choices, cases, and controversies explored in the earlier chapters shape how Americans can, if they want to, work to change our system of self-government today.

———

Exploring those issues is especially important right now. Those of us who care deeply about democratic self-government are being called upon for the first time in decades to defend principles we perhaps too casually assumed were both self-evident and shared. The turmoil of recent elections has revealed that many Americans are disillusioned with our institutions of government, frustrated by the inertia created by our elaborate system of checks and balances, and losing faith in elections as a reliable way to transfer political power.

But those same circumstances also have spurred a renewed interest in better understanding our electoral system and how we might improve it. The book speaks to that interest, by exploring the past to learn more about how we, the American voters, can answer Congressman Lewis's call and do our part to continue to shape the state of American democracy today.

One

Our Democratic Republic

We may define a republic to be, or at least may bestow that name on, a government which derives all of its powers directly or indirectly from the great body of the people, and is administered by persons holding their offices during pleasure, for a limited period, or during good behavior. . . . It is essential to such a government that it be derived from the great body of the society, not from an inconsiderable proportion, or a favored class of it.

—JAMES MADISON, Federalist 39, 1788

In America today, to call our system of government a "democracy" is to pick a fight with those who insist we are not a democracy, but a republic. Those on the "democracy" side of this argument highlight the importance of popular sovereignty, equality, and majority rule; those on the "republic" side emphasize checks on majoritarian power and judicial protection of individual rights.[1] But the distinction between the two is rarely as crisp as the most passionate participants in this debate assume. Consider the preceding quote from James Madison, one of the most respected men of the founding generation. A republic, he says, must derive all of its power, directly or indirectly, from the "great body of the people." Madison and his compatriots had a cramped view of "the people," but this idea was nonetheless both radical in its time and democratic at its core. In America, governmental power would be rooted not in the blood of a monarch or a hereditary aristocracy but rather in the ordinary citizens of the nation.

Debates about whether that makes us a democracy or a republic go back a long way.[2] In early America, the meaning of the terms "democracy" and "republic" were very much in flux.[3] Some members of the founding generation associated democracy with unconstrained majority rule and insisted (correctly) that we were not a "democracy" in that sense.[4] Others used the term "democracy" to describe what we today would call pure or "direct democracy," one in which all eligible citizens assembled and voted directly on the laws governing the nation.[5] "Republicanism," in turn, often was associated with a system in which the people's representatives governed with a sense of civic duty and public virtue seen as essential to responsible government.[6] But many others used the terms "democracy" and "republican" interchangeably to define systems, like ours, in which governing authority is derived from the people, not a king.[7] So, in a republic, the people would rule instead of a king, but they could do so directly in assemblies or indirectly through elected representatives. A republic, in other words, could be democratic in a deep and meaningful way.

The major questions our founders struggled with, consequently, were not whether we would be a democracy or a republic, as we define those terms today. Instead, their critical debates concerned how the institutions of a self-governing nation would be organized.[8] In democratic republics like ours, "the people" rule, but who *are* "the people" and *how* do they rule? In all but the smallest nations, direct democracy is not a viable way to govern a nation, so most actual lawmaking is done by the people's elected representatives. But that raises a host of questions. Representative democracy requires representatives, but who should be represented, and how?

Law professor Akhil Amar calls this the denominator problem.[9] Should the president of the United States be elected by a majority of voters across the nation, or by majorities within each state? Should every town, county, or state be equally represented, or should representation be distributed so all people are represented equally? If the latter, do children count? What about people who do not vote, or are not citizens? What about enslaved people, or people who live in the U.S. territories or the District of Columbia? The way a nation divides and allocates political representation is enormously consequential, but there rarely are obviously clear or self-evidently correct answers to questions like these.

Self-government also requires decisions about who "the people," however represented, actually are. "The people" of 1776 are, emphatically, not the people of today. In early America, enslaved people, free people of color, women, and Native Americans were routinely excluded from common understandings of the people entitled to participate in self-government.[10] Even white men without property were not immediately guaranteed the right to vote or hold office.[11] In most states today, children, people convicted of felonies, legal noncitizen residents, and undocumented immigrants continue to be excluded from the definition of the politically empowered people.[12] The exclusion from the franchise of each of these groups reflects different ideas about what self-government is, and who is entitled to exercise it.

Finally, self-government requires determining who gets to make key decisions about how the mechanics of self-government work. Elections don't run themselves. We need rules, and we have a lot of them. These rules govern everything from mundane issues like in what order candidates should be listed on the ballot to highly contested ones like where legislative district lines should be drawn. As we have seen in recent years, even "nuts and bolts" rules about things like voting by mail and ballot-counting procedures can become controversial in some contexts.[13] Yet despite their importance, it is not always obvious who should have the final say over what these rules are. The administration of elections in the real world raises countless questions under state and federal law, including both state and federal constitutional law. Consequently, many of our disputes about how our elections should work are really fights about who among the various actors in our system of self-government gets to *decide* how they work.

Questions like these—how to distribute representation, how to define "the people," and who gets to make the rules governing it all—are what this book is about. They also are the questions undergirding some of our most intense battles about what democracy in America should look like. Of all the different ways to define the people, distribute political power, and allocate public decision-making, which ones should we choose? As we will see in the following chapters, these questions are not new. Our predecessors struggled with them as well. Understanding the battles they fought and the choices they made (or in some cases failed to make) is essential to understanding the rules governing our democracy today and how we might change them if we want to.

So this book will begin at the beginning, by looking at two of the most important documents ever written about America's system of self-government: the Declaration of Independence and the 1787 Constitution. The Declaration of Independence was America's first official act as a self-proclaimed independent nation. The original Constitution of the United States, written in 1787 and effective in 1789, was the young nation's most consequential answer to the questions of who we are and how we will govern ourselves.

————

The Declaration of Independence is a remarkable document. Its sweeping proclamation that "all men are created equal" has inspired social movements at home and across the world. But in 1776, the Declaration was first and foremost what it announced itself to be: a declaration by the freemen of thirteen British colonies that they collectively had, and were asserting, the right to govern themselves as an independent nation.[14] The immediate importance of the Declaration to the early Americans, in other words, was not its rhetoric about the equality of men but its claim that the colonists were a distinct people, entitled to establish and ordain their own government rather than be ruled by someone else, from somewhere else.[15]

This concept of the sovereignty of the people—the right to govern ourselves—is the heart of the Declaration. For decades, colonial leaders in British America had enjoyed at least a modicum of self-government.[16] By 1776, each of the original colonies was governed by some combination of an executive appointed by the Crown and an upper or (more commonly) lower assembly elected by the freemen of each colony.[17] Men of means in the colonies had been electing representatives to this type of body since the 1600s.[18] These bodies were structured differently in different colonies, but their powers were not trivial. Maryland's colonial charter, for example, required all laws enforced by the royal governor to be consented to by the Maryland assembly.[19] Other assemblies had similar input into the laws governing their colonies.[20] In addition, local common-law courts resolved colonial disputes, and local governing bodies made the rules structuring much of the colonists' day-to-day life.[21]

Colonial leaders felt this was no less than their birthright as Britons, fully entitled to the same rights and privileges of self-government enjoyed by their counterparts in England.[22] This understanding had always been an uneasy one for a people separated from their government by a vast ocean, but the relative indifference of the British Parliament to colonial matters enabled it to prevail without serious challenge for decades.[23] That changed in the late 1700s. The responsibilities of an expanding empire led the British Parliament to take more interest in colonial matters, culminating, ultimately, in its insistence that it had power to govern (and tax) the colonies as it saw fit, no matter what the colonists thought about it.[24] That insistence made clear to the Americans that while they may have seen themselves as full and equal British citizens, their British cousins saw things quite differently.[25]

So they were understandably unhappy when the British began retrenching on the power-sharing arrangements they had long enjoyed. Historians have questioned the validity of many of the specific claims the Declaration raised against King George III,[26] but the text vividly captures the power of the rhetorical argument it wielded in favor of independence. The Declaration doesn't just demand independence for the colonists; it argues that the future Americans *deserved* it, because the king had deprived them of their right (as they saw it) to participate in how the colonies were governed.[27]

The first several items on the Declaration's list of accusations against the king all emphasize this complaint. According to the Declaration, he failed to respect the right of the colonists to have a voice in colonial assemblies; refused to assent to colonial laws and forbade the royal governors from doing so in his stead; demanded that the people relinquish their right to representation in colonial governing bodies and required those bodies to meet at "uncomfortable" places; dissolved representative assemblies and refused to permit the election of others; and denied the colonies permission to enact laws necessary for their safety and prosperity.[28] Claiming to have been deprived of these essential prerogatives of self-government, the freemen of the colonies revolted.[29]

How they did so illustrates the importance America has since the very beginning placed on the institutions of representative government. The men who signed the Declaration of Independence were not self-appointed rebels acting out their own personal grievances. They were representatives chosen by the colonial assemblies to gather at what came to be called the First Continental Congress and debate how the colonists, collectively, should respond to the actions of the British.[30] As delegates, they were closely tied to the assemblies that sent them. Some were given a free hand in deciding how to proceed, but many others were bound by "instructions" from their home assemblies limiting their authority and their response.[31]

All of which made our march toward declaring independence slow and methodical.[32] The delegates knew that the colonists were not yet united behind independence, and they also knew they could not outstrip the representative assemblies that had sent them.[33] While more impatient patriots were rattling the streets with revolutionary zeal, the delegates sent to the Continental Congresses understood that their role was to ground the colonists' claims in the institutions of collective self-government.[34] In a democratic republic like ours, "the people" may be sovereign but exercising that sovereignty in a concrete way requires representative institutions.[35] The men gathered in Philadelphia may have known that independence was where the nation was headed, and some probably wanted to nudge things in that direction.[36] But to act without authorization of the colonial assemblies would have been to betray what they said they were fighting for: the power of the people to govern themselves.

As the conflict intensified and support for independence grew, those restraints fell away. By late 1775, the British had escalated the conflict by suspending trade with the colonies and seizing American ships and property.[37] Fighting had already broken out in Massachusetts.[38] Across the colonies, individual citizens met and debated in their towns and counties, and colonial assemblies voted on the issue.[39] By June 1776 the delegates had the permission they had been waiting for. Every colony except New York (which seemed to be taking a wait-and-see attitude[40]) had formally supported declaring independence.[41]

Public support for independence was not universal, of course; nothing representative governments do ever is. A significant number of colonists remained loyal to the Crown, many of whom fled the country once war broke out.[42] Others were indifferent, or fickle in their preferences.[43] Nor did all the people in the colonies have a voice in the matter. Women, Native Americans, enslaved people, some white men without property, and free people of color were excluded from the franchise if not always the debates.[44] But the colonial assemblies, for all of their flaws, were the institutions through which the legitimacy of the Continental Congress flowed. So the delegates waited until they were armed with permission from the assemblies that had sent them. Only then, when they had those permissions in hand, did they issue the Declaration of Independence declaring America a free and independent nation.

This extended process illustrates a key point about democratic self-government, one we will return to throughout this book. Democracies, unlike monarchies, rest on the sovereignty of the people, but the people exercise that sovereignty through their elected representatives acting through their governing institutions.[45] In pre-revolutionary America, the signers of the Declaration of Independence could claim to speak on behalf of the people of the colonies because they could credibly claim to derive their authority from the elected colonial assemblies that sent them and approved their actions. That's why the men who signed the Declaration of Independence could do so "in the Name, and by the Authority" of the people of the colonies.[46] Given the Declaration's famous assertion that governments derive their just powers from the consent of the governed, this link to "the people" was essential to the integrity of their argument.

That means that in democratic republics like ours, how the institutions of representative government are designed, and who sits in them, are critical to how a nation's democracy actually works. The Declaration of Independence announced that the United States were free and independent but said nothing about how representative democracy in the new nation would actually function. That problem—how to design representative institutions of American government after independence—was the one our most famous founders had to grapple with a decade after the Revolutionary War, when they met to write our original 1787 Constitution. As we will see, in doing so, they confronted a daunting set of challenges.

———

The Revolutionary War brought the colonies together against a common enemy, but in 1776 those colonies were very much separate entities with distinct histories, values and needs.[47] The oldest of them, Virginia, was founded in 1607.[48] The newest, Georgia, was chartered more than a hundred years later in 1733.[49] Virginia and Massachusetts were established by mercantile corporations granted rights over the territory by the British crown, Pennsylvania was given to William Penn to settle a debt, and Rhode Island was founded by men banished from Massachusetts.[50] The colonies were not even all originally British. The Dutch were the first Europeans to establish permanent settlements in New York, while Sweden had been the first to lay claim to much of the mid-Atlantic region.[51] In addition, of course, many of the people in these spaces were not European at all.[52] A fifth of the people living in the colonies were enslaved and thousands were Native Americans.[53]

All of this meant that actual people living in the colonies in the wake of the Revolutionary War spoke dozens of languages, hailed from different regions of the world, practiced different religions, lived under different forms of government, enjoyed vastly different privileges, and bore decidedly different burdens.[54] How these people, the people who would become Americans, would organize and distribute political power in the new nation they had just fought to create was far from obvious. The first question they had to answer was perhaps the most fundamental: Were they creating a loosely connected confederation of independent states or a more fully unified new nation?

The closing sentences of the Declaration illustrate the problem:

> We, therefore, the Representatives of the united States of America, in General Congress, Assembled, appealing to the Supreme Judge of the world for the rectitude of our intentions, do, in the Name, and by the Authority of the good People of these Colonies, solemnly publish and declare, That these United Colonies are, and of Right ought to be Free and Independent States.

Read that last sentence again. What type of nation is this describing? One of "united colonies" or one of "independent states"?[55]

America's first national charter of government skewed heavily toward the latter interpretation. That charter was *not* the constitution written by James Madison and others in Philadelphia in 1787. Rather, our first founding charter was the Articles of Confederation, drafted by a committee appointed by the Second Continental Congress and adopted by that Congress in 1777.[56]

The government created by the Articles, unlike the Constitution that would follow it, truly was a federation of states, not a fully unified nation.[57] It was the state legislatures that ratified the Articles, and each state had equal representation in the national government regardless of population.[58] The national government also had very few areas in which it was authorized to act, and doing so even within those areas was difficult.[59] Most significantly, it had no direct power of taxation. It could raise money only by requisitioning funds from the states.[60] But federal authorities had no way to compel the states to honor the nation's financial obligations, and states often simply ignored congressional demands for payment.[61] In addition, the Articles were virtually impossible to change, because amending them required the unanimous consent of all thirteen states.[62] On the question of how to distribute representation and political power, in short, the Articles of Confederation landed firmly on the side of the state governments.

It didn't work. The Articles of Confederation lasted less than a decade.[63] States repeatedly refused to honor their financial obligations, leaving the new nation unable to pay either its foreign creditors or its military veterans.[64] Without any direct connection to the people, Congress had little ability to demand payments, and struggled to govern the nation with its limited powers.[65] A new system, with a stronger central government, was plainly needed.[66] So the states once again agreed to send delegates to Philadelphia, this time to discuss whether and how the Articles might be revised.[67]

The fifty-five men who met in Philadelphia in 1787 at what we now know as the Constitutional Convention included many of the most famous and respected men of the era.[68] George Washington oversaw the proceedings.[69] James Madison, who came armed with both a plan and a wealth of background research, was an active and fierce advocate of increasing the power of the central government.[70] Benjamin Franklin, Alexander Hamilton, George Mason, Gouverneur Morris, and James Wilson were all prominent participants. Other leading names of the time—Patrick Henry, John Jay, John Hancock, James Monroe, and Samuel Adams among them—played key roles in the state ratifying conventions that would follow.[71] Thomas Jefferson and John Adams were abroad on diplomatic assignments, but virtually every other man associated with the nation's founding participated directly in these processes, toiling over how to reconstitute the government to better serve the nation.[72]

They had a tough job. It was clear to everyone that a more powerful central government was needed, and that such a government would only be seen as legitimate if it had at least some direct accountability to the people it governed.[73] But that type of direct accountability posed its own problems. Early Americans supported self-rule—they had fought a war to preserve it, after all—but they also feared an "excess" of democracy.[74] Democracy requires the people be the source of political authority, but an empowered people may use that authority to engage in oppression or anarchy, especially when demagogues (who terrified the authors of the 1787 Constitution) succeed in inflaming and manipulating the people's anger and prejudice. Many of the men gathered in Philadelphia believed that the new state governments, which often were composed of relatively unconstrained legislators subject to frequent reelection and intense constituent pressures, were deeply problematic for precisely this reason.[75]

So the challenge presented by the failure of the Articles of Confederation was how to create a stronger central government in which the people were sovereign but within which they also were protected from abuse by unscrupulous masses and demagogues. This is a basic conundrum of democratic self-government: How do you empower the people while also constraining them? Monarchies and aristocracies control this particular risk (they obviously suffer from others) by severely restricting the number of people entitled to have a say in how their country is governed. But the founders of a nation built on the premise of popular sovereignty needed a different solution.

Today, there is a tendency to think of the solution to this problem as the entrenchment of constitutional rights in a written constitution protected by an independent judiciary. But that was not what lay at the heart of the founders' solution.[76] Their solution relied instead on designing a system of representative government that would channel the sovereignty of the people through competing institutions.[77] The overarching idea was to situate self-government within a protective framework composed of those institutions, each of which was itself representative of and responsive to different people in different ways.[78] Just how the proposed constitution would accomplish this was explored in a series of essays written by Madison, Hamilton, and Jay.[79]

Originally published in New York newspapers to support ratification of the freshly drafted constitution at that state's ratifying convention, we know these essays today as *The Federalist Papers*. Two of the most famous of the essays, Federalist 10 and Federalist 51, explain how the proposed constitution would both empower and constrain popular government. Both of these essays were written by James Madison, and they make similar points about how he expected (or perhaps hoped[80]) the new constitution would work. Federalist 10 does so by explaining why democracy can work in a large republic like the United States.[81] Federalist 51 does so by explaining the logic behind the constitution's extensive system of separation of powers.

In these essays, Madison tackles what he identifies as the problem of "factions"—the dangerous cabals that can capture the institutions of democratic government and use them to harm the public good. In Madison's words, a faction is "a number of citizens, whether amounting to a majority or a minority of the whole, who are united and actuated by some common impulse of passion, or of interest, adverse to the rights of other citizens, or the permanent and aggregate interests of the community."[82] As this definition makes clear, a faction can constitute either a majority or a minority of citizens. But Madison is not worried about minority factions because in a republican system of government, numeric minorities will simply be outvoted. Minority factions, he wrote, may "clog the administration" and "convulse the society," but the "republican principle" would allow the majority to defeat them by "regular vote."[83]

That means the real danger of self-government is the one presented by majority factions. Importantly, Madison's concern here is not about majoritarianism per se but rather about the problem of majority *factions*—those majority groups he believes are acting contrary to the public good.[84] (Madison glides over the thorny question of how to ascertain just what "the public good" is.) Classical political theory had long held that this problem meant democracy could only work, if at all, in small and relatively homogenous nations. Larger nations with more diverse populations, according to political theorists well-known to the founding generation, would contain people with so many divergent interests that they would splinter in pursuit of those interests rather than working collectively for the good of the whole.[85]

In Federalist 10, Madison turns that thinking on its head, arguing that a large republic like ours is in fact *better* suited to control factions than is a smaller republic. Not because factions won't develop in a larger republic (nothing but tyrannical rule could accomplish that[86]) but because large republics are more able to construct the type of representative institutions capable of controlling them. A large republic, Madison writes, requires larger legislative districts. Each of those (larger) districts will include a more diverse group of people with varied and competing interests. Representatives elected in those districts, therefore, will be accountable to *all* of these groups (factions), making it harder for any *one* of them to gain power. This effect, Madison continued, is then compounded across the nation. There will be so many competing factions in a large republic that even if a single interest dominated in one part of the country, oppressive coalitions among self-interested factional groups will be hard to build and impossible to sustain across the entire country.[87] Demagogues, he argued, will struggle in a large republic for the same reason. They may capture pockets of local support, but they won't be able to sway enough people enough of the time to win majority support across the nation.[88] In other words, the solution to factions, as Madison saw it, was more factions.[89]

Madison goes on to explain in Federalist 51 how separation of powers would control the risks of self-government in a similar way. As every American schoolchild learns, separation of powers is an essential part of the U.S. system of government. Our Constitution famously slices and dices political power in multitudes of ways. The federal government is divided into separate legislative, executive, and judicial branches, and each branch is itself occupied by officials who represent different constituencies, are elected in different ways, and hold their offices for different periods of times. Power is then further divided between the federal government and the governments of the states, which are themselves likewise composed of separate branches. As Madison put it, this elaborate division of power sets "ambition against ambition."[90] By locating the powers of government in so many different levels and branches, the individuals serving in the different bodies will check and balance each other by jealously guarding the prerogatives of their own institution. Separation of power protects the whole from the self-interested machinations of the parts.

But as Madison understood, doing that effectively requires powers to be not just separated but also overlapping. Without some overlap, power might be "balanced" but it could not be "checked."[91] The 1787 Constitution relies on this interconnectedness of institutions over and over again. The House of Representatives is directly elected by the people, but it can't enact legislation without the Senate, which (under the 1787 Constitution) was appointed by the state legislatures. The president can veto legislation passed by Congress, but Congress can override that veto with a supermajority vote. The justices of the Supreme Court determine the meaning of the Constitution and federal laws enacted under it, but they cannot take their seats until nominated by the president and confirmed by the Senate, and (like the president) they can be impeached and removed by Congress and are subject to other types of congressional regulation. As we will see in Chapter 3, both Congress and the states also play key roles in determining the process through which the president is chosen.

As he did in Federalist 10, Madison argues in Federalist 51 that the diversity and size of the American republic will help ensure the success of this elaborate system of separation of powers and checks and balances. The variety of interests in a large republic with multiple and competing levels of government will, he says, make it difficult for majority factions to form or sustain themselves. The language Madison uses in Federalist 51 to describe this idea is striking in light of some of today's discourse.

Often, the heterogeneity of American society is seen as a source of political conflict: Whether our differences make us stronger or weaker seems to be a perpetual debate in American politics. To Madison, it was a virtue.[92] It was the expansive and diverse (in 1787 terms) nature of the republic, he believed, that would work to protect the liberty of all. By including within a single, large nation people with widely disparate interests—by creating, as he put it, a society "broken into so many parts, interests, and classes of citizens"—the rights of all will be protected.[93] In other words, we sink or swim together.

————

So that's how the original Constitution set out to both constrain and empower democratic self-government. The sovereignty of the people celebrated in the Declaration of Independence would be channeled through the complex system of separation of powers and checks and balances built into the 1787 Constitution. That Constitution, unlike previous efforts at democratic self-government, would succeed in both empowering and controlling the people, and would do so not in spite of being a large republic but because of it. The institutions of American government would represent "the people" both directly and indirectly, through a complex web of competing centers of power populated by individuals elected by and accountable to voters with different interests and preferences. Because the republic would be large, self-interested factions and demagogues wouldn't be able to gain sufficient power to govern, and even if they did capture power in one place, the vastness of the republic meant no single self-interested faction could capture power across the entire nation. And even if that barrier failed, separation of powers among the three competing branches of the federal government, combined with the distribution of governing power between the federal government and the states, would further protect the best interests of the nation as a whole. Through the institutions of representative government established by the 1787 Constitution, the sovereignty of the people would be both honored and controlled.

So is that government a democracy or a republic? It is both, of course, and more. It is a democratic, representative, federalist, and constitutional republic. It is a democratic republic because it derives its authority from the people, not from a king or a hereditary aristocracy. It is a representative republic because we are governed by elected representatives who make policy choices on our behalf and who are accountable to us through regular elections. It is a federalist republic because governing power is divided not just horizontally between the branches of the national government but also between that government and the governments of the states.[94] And it is a constitutional republic because key choices about the structure of our government, as well as limitations on its powers, are set forth in a written constitution, capable of being amended, that is both the Supreme Law of the Land and designed to "endure for ages to come."[95]

The government created by the 1787 Constitution also, as its authors knew full well, was imperfect and riddled with compromises.[96] It failed to grapple with the divisive question of slavery, adopted a poorly thought-out mechanism for electing the president, and failed to appreciate how political parties would influence competition between the different levels and branches of government. Reasonable people also can (and do) disagree about whether Madison was correct that the design of our governing institutions can control the power of factions and demagogues. But whatever its flaws, the 1787 Constitution gave us the scaffolding on which all of our subsequent choices about our system of government would be built. Most of our disagreements about how to structure our system of self-government, consequently, have not been about whether to respect or disregard these various aspects of our constitutional design but rather about how to balance them. As we'll see in the next chapter, this is exactly what our predecessors had to do at the Constitutional Convention when they engaged in one of the nation's first great debates about how "the people" of the new nation would be represented in the halls of its government.

Two

Representing the People

Legislators represent *people*, not trees or acres. Legislators are elected by *voters*, not farms or cities or economic interests.

— CHIEF JUSTICE EARL WARREN, 1964[1]

This sentence, written by Earl Warren when he served as the Chief Justice of the United States Supreme Court, captures what many Americans think of as a fundamental tenet of democratic self-government. In a democracy, all people have an equal right to vote and be represented. We even have a catchy phrase for this idea: one person, one vote. But what does "one person, one vote" actually mean? Is representation and legislative power to be divided equally among people, or among voters? Chief Justice Warren's quote elides the differences between "people" and "voters," but they are not the same. Kids don't vote, but we count them when allocating representation. Should other nonvoters, perhaps noncitizen immigrants, count as well? Moreover, in the United States we plainly do not always represent either people *or* voters equally: The people of Washington, D.C. have no voting representation in Congress, each state has equal representation in the U.S. Senate regardless of population, and the Electoral College gives more power to voters in some states than others to elect the president of the United States.

CHAPTER TWO

These examples illustrate a basic fact about representative democracy. Representative government requires deciding whom to represent, how to group them together, and how to allocate political power among them. As we saw in the last chapter, a key strategy of the framers of the 1787 Constitution was to take advantage of this necessity to distribute representation and political power in multiple and overlapping ways. But they struggled over what that meant, in terms of who should be represented and how. This chapter examines those struggles and the profound impact that the choices made in 1787 have had on democracy in America today.

We'll begin by looking at the compromises made in the original Constitution about how to allocate representation in the U.S. Congress. We'll then examine two Supreme Court cases interpreting the Fourteenth Amendment to see how that amendment, enacted after the Civil War, has been interpreted to make political representation more equal across the nation. Finally, we'll turn to emerging efforts to reconsider those cases and, perhaps, to redistribute representation in America once again.

———

Article I of the 1787 Constitution establishes the U.S. Congress. Our Congress is bicameral, meaning it is divided into two chambers. In accordance with the design of the 1787 framers, representation in each of these chambers is distributed differently, and the members of each are elected by different groups of voters at different times. In the Senate, each state is represented by two senators regardless of the state's population, and senators are elected every six years by the voters of the state as a whole. In the House, representation is based on population. Each state is guaranteed at least one representative, but after that states with more people get more representatives, and each representative is elected by voters every two years in single-member districts drawn by the state legislature. As discussed shortly, the method of electing both senators and House members has changed over the years, but this basic structure has remained the same.

Today we tend to think of this scheme as embodying the framers' commitment to federalism and state sovereignty, but in 1787 it was one of the most hotly contested issues at the Constitutional Convention.[2] The first problem involved the design of the Senate. Far from expressing a deeply shared commitment to preserving state power, allocating two senators to each state regardless of population was not a particularly popular idea. James Madison, Alexander Hamilton, and many of the other better-known framers argued against giving states equal representation in even one house of the new Congress.[3] Madison also wanted senators to be directly elected by voters, rather than chosen by the state legislatures (as they were under the original Constitution).[4] To these men, a major problem of the Articles of Confederation was that the national government was too dependent on state legislatures.[5] They had little interest in re-creating that dynamic in the new system they were designing.

Delegates from states with large populations (or states that expected to see rapid population growth) also supported population-based apportionment of both chambers of Congress.[6] Assigning seats in both the House and the Senate on the basis of population would allow these states to elect more representatives to Congress, which would give them more power. Large-population states also worried that state-based representation would enable small-population states to use the national government's new powers to shift burdens to the larger states.[7] They particularly worried that small states could collude to impose high federal taxes that would be disproportionately paid by people in the larger-population states, which were also the wealthier states.[8] Finally, delegates from the large-population states understood that state-based representation would effectively give small-population states a veto over legislation favored by national majorities.[9] Such an arrangement, they argued, violated the republican principles of self-government they had fought for in the Revolutionary War.[10]

Delegates from small-population states saw things differently. They accused the large-population states of wanting to squash the rights of people living in small-population states. In a purely population-based system of representation, they argued, people living in the small states would be powerless in the face of the consolidated preferences of representatives from the large-population states.[11] They also insisted that the states, as existing sovereign entities, were entitled to be equally represented under the new constitution.[12] Finally, delegates from the small states argued that some form of state-based representation was necessary to preserve harmony between the states and the federal government.[13]

The debates around this issue were fierce and threatened to derail the entire project.[14] In the end, the small-population states won. In fact, they won so decisively that equal state representation in the Senate is one of only two parts of the 1787 Constitution that were written to be virtually unamendable (the other is the provision protecting the slave trade until 1808).[15] Their victory may have been inevitable. Equal state representation was the status quo under the Articles, and each state enjoyed equal representation at the Constitutional Convention itself.[16] The small states also seemed ready to walk away from the entire project if they didn't get their way.[17] So over the objections of Madison and others, the Convention adopted the so-called Great Compromise allocating representation in our bicameral legislature, with the House of Representatives composed of members elected on an equal population basis and the Senate composed of two senators from every state, chosen, until enactment of the Seventeenth Amendment in 1913, by the state legislature of the state.[18]

How to distribute representation within the House of Representatives presented a second challenge. Convention delegates quickly agreed that representation in the House, unlike the Senate, would be based on population.[19] It would be "the People's House"—the most democratic branch of the new government, directly elected by the people of the several states.[20] A census would be taken every decade, and House seats would be allocated to the states based on the population of each state. The larger a state's population, the more House seats it would get. How many would depend on the number of House seats Congress created (which is set by federal statute, not the Constitution[21]), but whatever seats were available would be distributed equally across the population.[22] The question that stymied the Convention delegates in their discussions about the House wasn't this basic structure but rather which "population" would count.

If the allocation of representation in the Senate provoked a fight between large- and small-population states, it was this question that set up a regional clash between northern and southern states.[23] The problem was slavery. As British colonies, slavery had been legal in each of the future states.[24] But in the hundred or so years between the establishment of the colonies and the Constitutional Convention, the pervasiveness of slavery had diminished in the north but exploded in the south.[25] By 1787, the enslaved population of several southern states matched or exceeded that of its white population.[26] In the northern states, in contrast, enslaved people rarely constituted more than 10 percent of any state's population.[27]

That set up a battle between the north and the south about whether enslaved people would count for purposes of apportioning seats in the House of Representatives.[28] Pause for a moment and imagine you are Charles Pinckney, an advocate for the interests of slaveholders and one of South Carolina's delegates at the Constitutional Convention.[29] In 1780, about 53 percent of South Carolina's population was enslaved.[30] If you were Pinckney, would you want that population to count for purposes of allocating South Carolina's House seats, or not? What would a person enslaved by Pinckney want?

The answer to this may be counterintuitive at first, but slaveholders like Pinckney argued that the people they enslaved *should* be fully counted when determining the population of each state for purposes of apportioning seats in the House of Representatives. Counting enslaved people as part of South Carolina's population would increase its power in the federal government. Because there was no expectation that representational or other rights would be given to enslaved people, counting them as part of the state's relevant population would increase the power of the enslavers, not the people they enslaved.[31]

We can illustrate this with an example. The only constitutional requirement governing Congress's choice of how many representatives sit in the House of Representatives is that each House district must include at least thirty thousand people.[32] Imagine that the first Congress set the total number of House seats at that minimum, and made the House just large enough for there to be one seat for every thirty thousand people. If South Carolina had a free population of sixty thousand and an enslaved population of ninety thousand, and if only the free population counted when apportioning House seats among the states, South Carolina would get two seats. But if the enslaved population also counted, then South Carolina would be entitled to *five* House seats. Since enslaved people were not allowed to vote, counting the enslaved population when apportioning House seats would more than double the power of South Carolina's free white population, giving them representation and power far exceeding their numbers among the free citizens of the nation.[33]

To many northern delegates, severing the distribution of political power from the actuality of political representation this way was unthinkable.[34] If enslaved people were not members of the political community, were not entitled to vote, and were not going to have their interests protected by the representatives elected by their "owners," why should their presence on southern soil be used to empower their enslavers?[35] Why should the vote of a southerner count for so much more, in such a system, than the vote of a northerner? The very idea was seen by many northern delegates as a betrayal of everything the new nation was supposed to stand for.[36]

Resolving this dispute required yet another compromise. It also led to the creation of one of the 1787 Constitution's more direct acknowledgments that the democratic republic it was creating was also a slaveholding republic. Captured in Article I, Section 2 of the 1787 Constitution, the Three-Fifths Compromise allowed enslaved people to be counted for purposes of apportioning seats in the House but only using a reduced ratio:

Representatives and direct Taxes shall be apportioned among the several States which may be included within this Union, according to their respective Numbers, which shall be determined by adding to the whole Number of free Persons, including those bound to Service for a Term of Years, and excluding Indians not taxed, three fifths of all other Persons.

Those "other Persons," of course, were slaves.

The Three-Fifths Compromise was proposed by Pennsylvania delegate and future Supreme Court Justice James Wilson.[37] Wilson's key move was to couple the issue of representation with that of taxation. Under the Articles of Confederation, the Congress of the Confederation assigned a certain portion of the nation's tax burden to each state. How much each state was responsible for depended on the state's population, with enslaved people counted using a three-fifths ratio.[38] Wilson leaned into that experience by once again relying on the three-fifths ratio, this time to determine both representation and taxation.[39] The 1787 framers expected the new government to continue to allocate the national tax burden among the states based on their population, through something called "direct" taxation.[40] Under Wilson's language, both direct taxes and representation would be apportioned using the three-fifths ratio. Voters in the slaveholding states would get more representation in the House relative to their northern peers, but they also would be subject to an equivalent increase in their share of the new national tax burden.

This solution was accepted by the delegates and ratified as part of the 1787 Constitution. But the deal did not work out quite the way they expected. Direct taxation turned out to be impractical and was rarely used by the new government.[41] So the compromise provided little value to the northern states.[42] But it yielded tremendous benefits for white southerners, who held disproportionate power in the national government up until the eve of the Civil War.[43] The Three-Fifths Compromise eventually was nullified by the Fourteenth Amendment, but even after that amendment was enacted, Black Americans living in the south remained unable to vote for decades, first as a legal and then as a practical matter.[44]

This meant that voters in the states where they lived continued to hold disproportionate sway over national politics long after the three-fifths clause itself was rejected.[45]

The 1787 Constitution and the Fourteenth Amendment also failed to clearly resolve yet another question of how to distribute representation and political power, one we are still arguing about today. Regardless of how seats in the House of Representatives are apportioned *among* the states, what constitutional rules govern how a state allocates its seats *within* the state? In other words, if the State of Georgia is allocated fourteen seats in the House of Representatives, what rules does the state have to follow in deciding how those fourteen members are elected and who they represent? Understanding what the Constitution has to say about this question requires us to take a deep dive into the 1960s, when the Supreme Court considered for the first time what, if any, constitutional constraints there are on how a state allocates representation among people within the state. The Court did so in the two groundbreaking cases we examine next: *Wesberry v. Sanders*[46] and *Reynolds v. Sims*.[47]

————

Wesberry was decided first. It involved how the State of Georgia drew the boundaries of its congressional districts. For several decades after the 1787 Constitution was adopted, many states elected members of Congress through what we would call "at large" elections.[48] In an at-large election, all voters in the state are presented with the same list of candidates and cast their ballots for candidates on that list. In some systems, each voter votes for just one candidate, and the available House seats are awarded based on how many votes each candidate received (so the first seat would go to the highest vote-getter, the next seat to the second-highest vote-getter, etc.).[49] In others, each voter votes for as many candidates as there are seats (so if there are five seats available, each voter can vote for five candidates on the list and then the top five vote-getters fill those seats).[50]

This changed in 1842, when Congress passed a law requiring states to elect House members through "single-member districts."[51] Single-member districts are what most Americans today are accustomed to. In single-member districts, a state is divided geographically into legislative districts and voters vote only for candidates running in their own district. After the ballots are cast, the candidate who gets either a majority (50 percent plus one) or a plurality (more than anyone else) of the votes in each district wins that district's seat.[52] It was this change that paved the way for the issue addressed by the Court in *Wesberry*. Single-member districts require decisions about how many people and which ones will reside in each district. That in turn creates the ability to manipulate the distribution of representation and political power within the state through strategic decisions about where to draw the lines.

The Georgia scheme challenged in *Wesberry* shows how.

After the 1930 census, Georgia was allocated ten seats in the House of Representatives.[53] It filled those seats by dividing the state into ten roughly evenly populated districts and electing one House member from each district.[54] It then kept that same districting plan in place for decades.[55] The problem was that during those intervening years, the number of people living in each of the districts had shifted and the population of the districts had become dramatically unequal. This was especially true in the Fifth District. The Fifth District centers on Fulton County and includes much of the city of Atlanta.[56] As counted in the 1960s census— thirty years after the districts were drawn—the Fifth District had a total population of 823,680 residents.[57] The average population of the other districts in the state was 394,312, less than half that of the Fifth.[58]

This disparity is what was challenged in *Wesberry*. The challengers were voters and residents of Fulton County.[59] Their complaint was that this extraordinary inequality violated the Constitution. To understand how, imagine two geographical areas, each with one hundred residents. The people living in one of these areas are lumped together into one single-member district and elect one representative. But the residents of the other area are divided into four single-member districts, each of which elects its own representative. In this scheme, the one hundred people in the second area enjoy *four times* the representational power that the people in the first area do, amplifying their interests at the expense of their neighbors. It takes the representational inequality built into the design of the Senate and replicates it in the House of Representatives.

States had recognized the unfairness of this approach when designing their own state legislatures.[60] Most of the original state constitutions adopted by the states required legislative districts in at least one chamber of the state legislature to be drawn in relation to population, and almost half required roughly equally populated districts in both chambers.[61] Courts did not always enforce these provisions, but the default position nonetheless was that most state legislative districts across the country were drawn to be at least somewhat population-proportionate.[62] But that began to change in the early 1900s. The industrial revolution brought rapid growth in urban areas.[63] These growing cities were often populated by people to whom the existing elites were unwilling to yield power.[64] All of this made state legislators reluctant to draw new district lines that would redistribute political power to these groups or harm their own reelection chances.[65] The net effect was that both state and congressional districts in many states, like Georgia, had become extremely unequally populated.[66]

The difficulty for the Fulton County challengers was how this becomes a constitutional issue. There are two separate court systems in the United States: state courts and federal courts. Generally speaking, state courts decide issues of state law and federal courts decide issues of federal law, including issues arising under the U.S. Constitution.[67] What the Fulton County challengers wanted was for the U.S. Supreme Court (a federal court) to invalidate a Georgia law (the state law drawing the state's congressional districts). The problem was that no federal law prohibited population-malapportioned congressional districts. Congress had mandated that states use single-member districts when drawing those districts, but neither that law or any other federal statute required them to include an equal number of actual people.[68] Nothing in the U.S. Constitution explicitly required equally populated districts either. So the first thing the challengers in *Wesberry* had to do was identify what part of the federal Constitution they were relying on to argue that unequally populated House districts were not just unfair but also unconstitutional.

Their answer to that question returns us to the language of the original Constitution. Article I, Section 2 of the 1787 Constitution says that the House of Representatives shall be chosen "by the people" of the several states.[69] We saw earlier how the "several states" portion of that language organizes the apportionment of available House seats among the states. The Fulton County challengers focused on the part of the provision mandating that House members be chosen "by the people." The "by the people" language of Article I is the closest thing the U.S. Constitution has to an express guarantee of a basic right to vote. After all, how would "the people" select House members except by voting for them?

The Fulton County challengers embraced that reading, and then they went further. Election by "the people," they argued, meant election by all of the people, equally. The right to vote for House members, they said, necessarily includes the right to have your vote carry what they described as the same "weight" as your neighbor's.[70] A districting scheme that instead gave people in less populated districts more representational power than it gave to people in more populated districts violated this principle, and was, they argued, unconstitutional.[71]

The Supreme Court agreed. Justice Hugo Black, writing for the majority, grounded the Court's decision in both the text and history of Article I.[72]

Textually, the Court said that the command that House members be chosen by the people meant that "as nearly as is practicable one man's vote in a congressional election is to be worth as much as another's."[73] In reaching that conclusion, the Court drew an analogy to a statewide election, like that for governor. It would be extraordinary in such an election, Justice Black wrote, to allow a state to give more weight to the votes of only those people living in certain areas of the state. Unequally populated legislative districts, he went on, had the same effect and should be likewise prohibited. To hold otherwise, Black concluded, would "not only run counter to our fundamental ideas of democratic government, it would cast aside the principle of a House of Representatives elected 'by the People.'"[74]

The Court's historical argument reached back to the Constitutional Convention. Justice Black noted that the election of House members by the people had been "tenaciously fought for" at the Convention, and that representational equality was at the heart of these disputes.[75] "Repeatedly," Black wrote, "delegates rose to make the same point: that it would be unfair, unjust, and contrary to common sense to give a small number of people as many Senators or Representatives as were allowed to a much larger group."[76] Black cited James Madison's insistence on the direct election of representatives "in proportion to their numbers"; James Wilson's argument that "equal numbers of people ought to have an equal no. [sic] of representatives"; and the assertion of George Mason (a Virginia delegate) that the "larger branch" of Congress was to be "the grand depository of the democratic principle of the Government."[77]

This history, Black wrote, made it "abundantly clear" that when the Convention delegates decided that seats in the House of Representatives would be apportioned among the states based on total population, they also intended that the representatives holding those seats would each represent an equal number of people.[78] It would "defeat the principle solemnly embodied in the Great Compromise," Black wrote, "for us to hold that, within the States, legislatures may draw the lines of congressional districts in such a way as to give some voters a greater voice in choosing a Congressman than others."[79] The People's House was to represent the people, equally.

The Court's decision in *Wesberry v. Sanders* ensured that congressional districts would be equally populated. But that was only half the battle for representational equality in America's legislative bodies. Article I governs how congressional districts are drawn but doesn't say anything about how state legislatures elect their *own* members—the elected representatives who sit in state assemblies and state senates across the country.

The same forces that led congressional districts like Georgia's Fifth to become grossly unequally populated had created the same disparities in these state legislative districts. But Article I's mandate that the House be elected "by the people" is about Congress. It does not speak to the election of representatives to state legislatures. So what, if any, provisions of the U.S. Constitution might guarantee representational equality in those bodies?

That was the question the Court faced in our next case, *Reynolds v. Sims*.[80] *Reynolds* was decided the same year as *Wesberry*. It involved the apportionment of the Alabama state legislature.[81] The challengers were voters from Jefferson County, Alabama, near Birmingham. The Alabama state constitution did not require equally populated state legislative districts.[82] Instead, Alabama's constitution did something quite different: It required that each county in the state be represented by at least one state representative *and* one state senator.[83] Because counties across Alabama contained vastly different numbers of people, this created unequally populated districts. The disparities were huge. Jefferson County contained a whopping forty-one times as many people as did other districts in the state.[84]

Generally speaking, states can (and must) follow their own state constitutions. But if a state constitutional provision conflicts with the U.S. Constitution or any other valid federal law, then the state rule has to give way.[85] In *Wesberry*, the federal law that invalidated the Georgia scheme was Article I of the Constitution. But because the Alabama districts challenged in *Reynolds* involved the Alabama state legislature rather than the representatives Alabama sent to the House of Representatives, voters in Jefferson County could not rely on Article I or *Wesberry* for a remedy. They needed a different argument.

They found one in the Fourteenth Amendment. The Fourteenth Amendment is one of three constitutional amendments adopted by the Reconstruction-era Congress and ratified after the Civil War.[86] These amendments, especially the Fourteenth, fundamentally altered the relationship between the federal government and the states. Unlike the 1787

Constitution, which left the relationship between states and the people living within them largely to state law, the Fourteenth Amendment for the first time put the full power and protection of the federal Constitution between people and the states in which they lived. It also is the main constitutional vehicle for ensuring the equal rights of all Americans.

The Jefferson County challengers grounded their argument in Section 1 of the Fourteenth Amendment, which states:

> No state shall make or enforce any law which shall abridge the privileges or immunities of citizens of the United States; nor shall any State deprive any person of life, liberty, or property, without due process of law; nor deny to any person within its jurisdiction the equal protection of the laws.

We will look more closely at this language in Chapter 5. For current purposes, the question presented in *Reynolds* was whether the unequally populated state legislative districts drawn by Alabama violated this provision by denying people in higher-population districts the "equal protection" of the laws. If Article I of the Constitution required representational equality in the House of Representatives, then surely, the challengers argued, the federal guarantee of equal treatment under law provided by the Fourteenth Amendment protected the same representational equality in state legislative chambers.

Once again, the Supreme Court ruled in favor of the voters, requiring for the first time that districts for virtually all elected legislative bodies in the United States be equally populated. But because the constitutional foundation of the claim was different than in *Wesberry*, the Court's reasoning was different as well. The Court's decision, written by Chief Justice Earl Warren (and the source of the quote opening this chapter) relied on three arguments.

First the Court recognized that voting is "fundamental" in a democratic society.[87] The Supreme Court's fundamental rights doctrine is complicated, but the basic idea is that certain rights, especially those reflected in our history and traditions or essential to what the Court calls "ordered liberty," are so important that a state cannot unduly burden

them or take them away without a compelling reason.[88] The Supreme
Court first identified voting as a fundamental right in *Yick Wo v. Hopkins*,
decided in 1886.[89] In *Yick Wo*, the Court explained that voting was fundamental because it is the most basic way we are able to preserve all of
our other rights (by aligning with other voters and electing representatives we believe will best protect the things we care about).[90]

Reynolds built on this reasoning, arguing that since doing this on
equal terms as your fellow citizens is a core component of democratic
equality, any deviation from equality in the voting realm must be viewed
skeptically, and would rarely be justified.[91] State legislatures, the Chief
Justice wrote, are "the fountainhead of representative government" and
therefore should be responsive to the popular will.[92] That, in turn, meant
that the aim of legislative apportionment should be "the achieving of fair
and effective representation of all citizens."[93] The *Reynolds* Court did not
attempt to fully define "fair and effective" representation but concluded
that the Equal Protection Clause required, at a minimum, that all votes
carry equal weight in the election of state legislators.

Next, the Court considered the particular justification Alabama of-
fered in defense of its system, namely, that it wanted to ensure the equal
representation of counties rather than of people. This defense raises the
essential question of who (or what) state legislators are supposed to represent. Are state legislatures more like the House of Representatives—the
People's House—where individuals are entitled to equal representation,
or the U.S. Senate, where it is a unit of government (states) that are represented equally? Chief Justice Warren, writing for the majority, answered
this question emphatically in favor of the people. Legislatures, as he famously wrote, represent people, not trees, acres, or land.

But as Warren realized, there is a problem with this reasoning: It
is at odds with the structure of the U.S. Senate. If democratic equality
under our constitutional system requires equality of individuals rather
than regions or interests, why does the Constitution sanction state-based
representation in the Senate?[94] Warren addressed this issue in his third
and final argument. In doing so, he again went back to 1787 and the

Constitutional Convention. When the 1787 framers designed the original Constitution, he wrote for the Court, they were working within a unique set of constraints. They had to design a system that would strengthen the federal government, keep small- and large-population states on board, and placate regional jealousies and suspicions.[95] That required them to make compromises, and one of those compromises (the Great Compromise) was the composition of the U.S. Senate.

But no similar need exists, Warren reasoned, when deciding how to distribute representation within the states. Unlike the original states, cities, counties, and acres of land do not have any interests that need to be compromised away at the cost of democratic equality.[96] They are mere creatures, or subunits, of states, created by state constitutions.[97] They are not and never have been sovereign entities. So while state legislatures like Alabama's may *want* to give more power to rural voters than urban voters, or treat all counties equally rather than all people, that interest simply is not compelling enough to burden the fundamental constitutional right, protected by the Equal Protection Clause, of all Alabama residents to be represented in their government on equal terms as their neighbors.[98]

————————

Combined, *Wesberry* and *Reynolds* stand for the proposition, promised in the Declaration of Independence and the 1787 Constitution, and more fully realized after the Civil War, that all Americans have the right to participate as equals in our democracy. But even though these cases were decided more than half a century ago, some of the issues they invoke about how to allocate representation remain surprisingly unsettled.[99] This includes one of the most basic questions presented by the Court's "one person, one vote" rule. Under *Wesberry* and *Reynolds*, legislative districts must be equally populated, but what population must be equalized? Is it people, or voters?[100]

Shockingly, the Supreme Court avoided dealing with this basic issue until 2016, when it finally confronted it in a case called *Evenwel v. Abbott*.[101] Like *Reynolds*, *Evenwel* involved a challenge to a state legislative districting plan, this time involving state senate districts in Texas. In drawing the state senate district lines, Texas did what virtually all states have done since *Reynolds*: It created districts containing equal numbers of people.[102] This included all the people actually living in the districts, including kids, noncitizen permanent residents, undocumented immigrants, and other nonvoters.[103] The challengers in *Evenwel* claimed that this was the wrong population to count. They argued that the Equal Protection Clause instead required Texas to draw districts keyed in some way to *voters*, either by equalizing the number of eligible voters in each district or, alternatively, by equalizing the citizen voting-age population of each district (because citizens can sometimes lose their eligibility to vote, these measures will be similar but not identical).[104]

Using the language of *Wesberry* and *Reynolds*, the Texas challengers argued that equalizing districts based in some way on voters rather than people was the only way to ensure that their votes would not be undervalued relative to those of others. When nonvoters (like children and noncitizens) are evenly distributed across a state, the voters-versus-people distinction makes little difference.[105] But nonvoters in Texas were not evenly distributed. The total resident population of the Texas senate districts deviated by around 8 percent. But if the districts were instead compared using their citizen voting-age population rather than their total resident population as the relevant denominator, they had a population deviation of up to 40 percent—well beyond what the Supreme Court has said is acceptable. So the question presented in *Evenwel* was what population does the Equal Protection Clause require states to equalize? Do all people count as part of the relevant population, or only some of them?[106]

State legislatures redistricting after *Reynolds* and *Wesberry* had for the most part used all people—the total population living in a district—as the population to be equalized.[107] That is the population counted every decade by the U.S. Census and is the information most readily available to the states.[108] As we've seen, it also is the population that counts when House seats are allocated among the states.[109] The text of the Equal Protection Clause likewise extends its protection to all people, not just citizens.[110] But as the challengers in *Evenwel* correctly pointed out, *Reynolds* itself talks about voters and citizens, not just people and populations.[111] So there appeared to be no clear answer to the question of what population states are required to equalize when distributing representation within the state.

As it turns out, the Court's decision in *Evenwel* doesn't quite answer that question either. The *Evenwel* lawsuit had been brought by eligible voters in Texas against the Texas governor and secretary of state.[112] That meant that all Texas had to do to win the case was show that what it had done—equalizing the total number of actual people living in each district—was a constitutionally permissible option. Since that is what states had done for more than half a century, this was not a difficult argument for Texas to make. The challengers, on the other hand, had a much trickier case. For them to win, they had to convince the Supreme Court that the Constitution required all states, including Texas, to change their existing practices and equalize districts based on a completely different measure. In other words, Texas was defending its right to *choose* to use total population as the relevant denominator, while the challengers were claiming that using *anything other* than their preferred method violated the Constitution.

In one sense, then, *Evenwel* was an easy case. All states today use the total number of people residing in a district as the thing that needs to be equalized across legislative districts.[113] The posture of *Evenwel* allowed the Court to decide nothing more than that this decades-old practice is not prohibited by the Constitution, which is exactly what the justices did. This limited holding, though, means that *Evenwel* did not answer the basic question it presented about who should be represented, and why. That virtually ensures that the issue of what population can be equalized in legislative bodies across the country districting will come back to the Supreme Court sooner rather than later.

———

Several states are already testing these waters. Since *Evenwel* was decided, elected officials in Texas, Arizona, and elsewhere have embraced efforts in their states to count only voting-age citizens when drawing equally populated legislative districts.[114] Other states, most notably North Carolina, are pushing the Court to reconsider *Reynolds* by introducing "Little Federal Model" bills that mimic the design of Congress by allocating representation in the upper house of the state legislature by county rather than population, overrepresenting less populated rural areas at the expense of more densely populated urban and suburban areas.[115] These disputes are today's manifestation of the same issues our founders faced when struggling with how to distribute representation and political power in the original Constitution. Like the three-fifths clause and the composition of the Senate, proposals to only count citizens or voters when allocating representation or to give counties equal representation in statehouses rest on contested ideas about who deserves representation and why.

When nonvoters are counted as part of the population being equalized in a legislative district, the relative weight of the votes cast in their district increases relative to the weight of votes cast by voters in populations with fewer nonvoting residents: the nonvoters' parents, neighbors, allies, or in some cases political opponents gain representational weight by the inclusion of nonvoters in the population denominator. Whether this strikes us as fair depends in large part on whether we think the specific nonvoters at issue deserve to have their interests represented (like kids), and if so whether we believe the people in their district who *are* empowered to vote will actually do so (unlike slaveholders).

Providing equal representation in state legislatures to counties rather than people has a similar weighting effect and rests on similarly contested ideas about who deserves representation and why. By diminishing the representation of urban and suburban residents, these proposals would make legislative bodies less representative of the population as a whole in order to provide more representation to voters who vote in lower-population counties. Whether that seems appropriate is likely to rest on whether we think the interests of those voters or units of government are unique or otherwise worthy of disproportionate representation in our system of self-government.

Supporters of proposals like these often justify this redistribution of political power by claiming the mantle of the 1787 framers (consider the term "Little Federal Model"), but the compromises discussed in this chapter should give supporters of such proposals pause. The main architect of the constitution, James Madison, accepted nonmajoritarian devices like the Senate only reluctantly, as the necessary price of getting rid of the reviled Articles of Confederation. And while the original framers may not have shared our understanding of who the people entitled to participate in self-government are, they plainly understood majority rule as an essential component of republican government (consider Madison's expectation in Federalist 10 that minority factions could be controlled through the regular functioning of representative government). As we will see in the next chapter, the founders' commitment to majoritarianism even plays an important role in how they expected presidents to be elected under the complex Electoral College system. The overrepresentation of some voters at the expense of others is at times the consequence of the choices they made, but it was rarely the point.

The nonmajoritarian compromises of the original Constitution also look very different today than they did in 1787. In 1787, a voter from the least populous state (Delaware) had about twelve times the voting power in the Senate of a voter in the most populous state (Virginia).[116] Today, that ratio is a stunning seventy times between the smallest-population state (Wyoming) and the largest (California).[117] The inequitable nature of the U.S. Senate is even more extreme when we take into account the more than half a million Americans living in Washington, D.C. who have no representation in the Senate at all. More fundamentally, our nation's debates about how to divide representation and political power did not end in 1787. The Fourteenth Amendment gave more Americans the right to equal citizenship under law, and the Supreme Court's decisions in *Wesberry* and *Reynolds* told us that equal citizenship includes the right to at least some form of equal representation in legislative bodies. All these choices, not just those made in 1787, are part of the story of representative democracy in America, and all need to be part of the conversation when thinking about how to distribute representation and political power today.

That is particularly important to remember in our system, because the Senate is not the only branch of the federal government that fails to equally represent Americans: Our strange way of electing a president can have that effect as well. How we ended up with *that* system involves a completely different set of choices, which is where we will turn our attention next.

Three

Electing the President

Wise and virtuous as were the members of the Convention, experience has shown that the mode therein adopted cannot be carried into operation; for the people do
not elect a person for an elector who, they know, does not
intend to vote for a particular person as President.

—COMMENTS OF A MEMBER OF CONGRESS,
as reported in the *Congressional Record*, 1802[1]

Early in the morning on March 4, 1801, President John Adams walked
out of the White House and went home. This ordinary act was, in fact,
extraordinary. Adams had served two terms as George Washington's
vice president, followed by a single term as president. He had been an
integral part of the executive branch literally since its inception. But in
the election of 1800, he lost the top spot to his political nemesis (and
vice president!) Thomas Jefferson. The loss marked the first time in the
nation's history that the reigning political party, the Federalists, would
lose control of the government they had been so instrumental in creating.
President Washington gets well-deserved accolades for voluntarily relin-
quishing power by declining to run for a third term, but it is Adams who
showed us how the peaceful transfer of power through elections would
work, by the simple act of going home.[2]

It could have played out very differently. The election of 1800 was messy. Adams and Jefferson had emerged as leaders of two very different political movements, each claiming to represent the principles fought for in the Revolution and formalized in the Constitution. Adams's Federalists were allied with George Washington and viewed themselves as the natural guardians of the republic. Jefferson's Democratic-Republicans[3] believed the Federalists had betrayed the values of the Revolution and were leading the nation toward aristocracy, or even back to monarchy.[4] Neither really saw the other as legitimate political opponents.[5] Political competition as we know it today—political organizations building coalitions, competing for votes in contested elections, and routinely transferring power—was just emerging, and the idea of the "loyal opposition" had not yet fully taken hold on this side of the Atlantic.[6]

In the election of 1800, that distrust ran straight into one of the strangest parts of our Constitution: the way we elect our president. This set of procedures, which we collectively refer to as the Electoral College (a term that does not appear in the Constitution) resulted in a situation in which the Democratic-Republican choice for president (Jefferson) ended up in an electoral vote tie *not* with his Federalist opponent, John Adams, but instead with his own party's choice for vice president, Aaron Burr. That meant neither Jefferson nor Burr, and certainly not Adams, had the electoral votes constitutionally required to win the presidency. Under Article II of the Constitution, when the electoral vote is tied or when no candidate wins a majority of the votes (meaning more than 50 percent, rather than just more than anyone else), the selection of the winner is kicked to the House of Representatives, where the delegation of each state casts a single vote for president on behalf of their state.

Under the election timelines as they existed in 1800, the new House had not yet been sworn in to office when the electoral votes were counted, which meant the new president would be chosen by the lame-duck House rather than the recently elected one. A majority of those old members were Federalists, many of whom had been defeated in the November election.[7] But while the outgoing Federalists had a majority of members in the House, they did not control a majority of the state delegations. The Federalists comprised a majority of six state delegations, the Democratic-Republicans controlled eight, and two (Vermont and Maryland) were equally divided.[8] So even though the Democratic-Republicans controlled more state delegations than the Federalists, they also didn't control a majority of them. That was a problem, because as with the electoral vote count, the winner of the vote in the House had to win a majority of votes, not a mere plurality. All of which meant the defeated Federalists had in their hands the power to determine who would become the next president, even though their candidate had come in third in the electoral vote count, even though a majority of the electors had intended to elect Jefferson as president and Burr as vice president, and even though the Democratic-Republicans had routed the Federalists so badly in the November elections that the party would never again be a major player in national politics.

Jefferson's supporters were outraged. The governors of Pennsylvania and Virginia called up their state militias and vowed to march on Washington if necessary to protect Jefferson's victory.[9] The Federalists, in turn, entertained various maneuvers to defeat Jefferson. They considered brokering a deal with Burr to share power in a Burr administration, calling a new election, and extending debate beyond the constitutional deadline for choosing a new president.[10] For days no candidate could garner the required nine (of sixteen) votes necessary to win a majority of the state delegations.[11] Finally, after thirty-five rounds of balloting and an apparent intervention from Alexander Hamilton (who was a political opponent of Jefferson but detested Burr[12]), Federalists in the Delaware caucus voted to abstain.[13] That started a retrenchment that eventually led key representatives from the tied states of Vermont and Maryland to change course as well and cast their ballots for Jefferson. Only then did Jefferson finally have the votes he needed to be elected president.[14]

How could something as important as electing a president go so wrong so quickly? This chapter explains the original Electoral College design, why the 1787 framers settled on it from among several options debated at the Constitutional Convention, and how it was almost immediately amended. It then looks at how changes to both state and federal laws have affected how the process works in practice. Finally, the chapter considers arguments for and against retaining the Electoral College system, and explains the most viable alternatives.

———

The American way of electing our chief executive officer is unlike anything used anywhere else in the world, or even anywhere else in our own country. Rather than have the one elected official tasked with representing the people of the nation as a whole elected by the voters of the nation as a whole, we choose our chief executive through a complicated, indirect system.

The Electoral College system as originally designed is set out in Article II, Section 1 of the 1787 Constitution, which begins:

> Each State shall appoint, in such Manner as the Legislature thereof may direct, a Number of Electors, equal to the whole Number of Senators and Representatives to which the State may be entitled in the Congress: but no Senator or Representative, or Person holding an Office of Trust or Profit under the United States, shall be appointed an Elector.

This text immediately reveals several important things about how we elect the president. First, *we* don't—the "electors" do. The electors are exquisitely ephemeral. Every four years, they are chosen, cast their votes, and then disperse. They have no other constitutional duties and play no other constitutional role. Second, the number of electors allocated to each state tracks the allocation of representation among the states. Each state is assigned a number of electors equal to the number of members it sends to Congress. So each state gets two electors corresponding to its two senators, plus an additional number of electors equal to its seats in the House. That means the population disproportionality embodied in the structure of the Senate is partially replicated in the Electoral College. Finally, each state gets to determine for itself how its electors are chosen;

there is no single, federally mandated method states must use when choosing their electors. Today all states choose their electors through a popular vote within the state, but as we will see that has not always been the case.

The 1787 framers weren't all sold on this system (James Madison said it was the result of "hurrying influence, produced by fatigue and impatience"[15]) and considered several options before settling on it. Some delegates at the Constitutional Convention argued that the president should be elected directly by the people, through a national popular vote.[16] But this raised concerns about whether voters in far-flung states would know enough about candidates outside their own region to cast their votes knowledgably, or whether instead they would just cast their votes for their own state's "favorite sons."[17] Southern delegates also were skeptical of a direct national popular vote, because the northern states had more white men—the people who would vote in a national popular election—than did the slaveholding states.[18] Some small-population states objected for the same reason.[19] So direct election through a national popular vote never garnered the support of a majority of delegates.[20]

The delegates also considered having either Congress or the state legislatures choose the president.[21] But there were objections to these methods as well. A chief executive dependent on Congress for his position would lack the independence needed to check congressional power. That concern became especially acute after the delegates changed the presidential tenure in office from a single seven-year term to four-year terms with the possibility of reelection.[22] Selection by the state legislatures was unpopular for similar reasons. The purpose of drafting a new constitution, after all, was to create a federal government free from the stifling control that states had exercised over it under the Articles of Confederation.[23] Allowing state legislatures to choose the president would stymie that goal. So these proposals also gained little traction.

In the end, the delegates couldn't resolve their differences and referred the question to the aptly named Committee on Unfinished Parts.[24] The committee came up with a system that, after a few tweaks, is the one we are familiar with today. Rather than empower any single entity to select the president, this compromise allowed voters, states, and Congress to all play a role.[25] Voters wouldn't elect the president directly through a nationwide popular vote, but the allocation of electoral votes was made at least somewhat proportionate to population by distributing electoral votes among the states on the basis of a state's total congressional representation (the House as well as the Senate). State legislatures wouldn't get to select the president but were given power to decide how their state's electors would be chosen. And Congress got the so-called contingent election process that kicks in when no candidate receives a majority of electoral votes, shifting the decision to the House, where, as happened after the election of 1800, each state casts a single ballot until someone wins a majority.

How this works in practice today is that state legislatures in each state have enacted laws establishing how their state's electors will be chosen. All states now do this through some form of popular vote within the state.[26] State law also assigns political parties in the state the task of naming a slate of potential electors pledged to vote for their party's candidate.[27] States can, and frequently do, require electors to cast their electoral votes consistent with their pledge, and reserve the right to fine or replace electors who fail to do so.[28] Voters in the state then cast their ballots, and the slate of electors pledged to the winning candidate becomes the state's official slate of electors. Those electors meet at a designated time and place and cast the state's electoral votes. Their votes are certified by the appropriate state officials and sent to Washington to be counted at a joint session of Congress. That joint session is presided over by the president of the Senate, who under Article 1 of the Constitution is usually the sitting vice president. The votes are counted, the new president is chosen, and the old one goes home.

––––––––

At least that is how it is supposed to work. Yet in 1800, Thomas Jefferson ended up in an Electoral College tie with his own running mate. Understanding how the Constitution's original design led to this result requires returning to the text of Article II to gain a better understanding of the role originally assigned to the presidential electors.

Article II, Section 1, Clause 3 of the 1787 Constitution reads as follows:

> The Electors shall meet in their respective States, and vote by Ballot for two Persons, of whom one at least shall not be an Inhabitant of the same State with themselves. And they shall make a List of all the Persons voted for, and of the Number of Votes for each; which List they shall sign and certify, and transmit sealed to the Seat of the Government of the United States, directed to the President of the Senate.

Once again, several things about this text are immediately interesting. We see how the 1787 framers' concern about "favorite sons" generated the requirement that at least one vote cast by each elector must be for someone not from the elector's home state. This text also reveals a common misperception about the Electoral College: this "college" has never met, and was never intended to meet, as a group. Instead, each state's electors convene in their own state and cast their votes. But the most striking thing about this text is in the first sentence. Each elector casts *two* votes, with no designation delineating the votes cast for the president and vice president. Instead, each elector just votes for two people, then "the person having the greatest number of votes" (assuming a majority) is elected president and the next highest vote-getter is elected vice president.

In the first two presidential elections (1788 and 1792), casting undesignated votes this way made no difference in the presidential election. All of the electors in both of those elections cast one of their votes for George Washington, the consensus candidate to lead the nation.[29] So the only real uncertainty in those years was who would receive a majority of the electors' second votes and thereby be elected vice president. But the third presidential election, in 1796, was different. Washington wasn't running, so for the first time there was real competition for the top spot. Adams won a majority of the electoral votes, but the second-place vote-getter was none other than Jefferson, the leader of the emerging opposition party. So our first truly contested presidential election resulted in a president and vice president who were leaders of opposing political movements.[30]

As awkward as that must have been, as we have seen it was about to get worse. By 1800, both the Federalists and the Democratic-Republicans had begun coordinating their electoral efforts with their political allies, including by specifying which of their candidates they were supporting as president and which as vice president.[31] They hoped this would help them win both offices and avoid a repeat of 1796. The Federalists supported Adams for president and South Carolinian Charles Cotesworth Pinckney for vice president. The Democratic-Republicans wanted Jefferson for president and Burr for vice president.[32] The Federalists, though, smartly arranged for one of their electors to cast their second vote for someone *other* than Pinckney. That way, if a majority of the electors supported the Adams/Pinckney ticket, Adams would come in first and Pinckney would come in second.[33] But the Democratic-Republicans made no such arrangement. Each of their electors cast one vote for Jefferson and one vote for Burr.[34] Which is how Jefferson and Burr ended up tied.

Why would the 1787 framers have designed a process like this? In part, because they needed to settle on something and this system was the least objectionable to the most delegates.[35] But their failure to anticipate the particular problem revealed in the election of 1800 had a more specific cause. The original framers didn't anticipate the role political parties would almost immediately play in American politics.[36] In 1787, most political elites expected that voters would pay little attention to national politics and instead would cast their votes based on the reputation and character of the individuals they were asked to vote for.[37] When the election was over, the people, having had their say, would defer to the policy choices of their chosen representatives.[38] The role of the good voter was to choose wise representatives and then leave them alone to govern as they saw fit.[39]

In a system organized around this view of politics, the original Electoral College made some sense. Voters would have little direct knowledge of most presidential candidates and would not be well-suited to evaluate their fitness for office. So instead they would vote for electors from their own state, whose character and reputation they were more acquainted with. Those men would then use their own judgment to determine how to cast the state's electoral votes, and the two most worthy men would lead the nation as president and vice president. But this vision of politics failed to account for democratic expectations taking root across the country.[40] It turned out that people who threw off a king in the name of self-government were not eager to cede that government to a different group of elite leaders. Instead, they were busy forming political associations, demanding voting rights, and generally throwing themselves into the work of self-government.[41]

Emerging political parties channeled this energy by giving people a way to actively engage with the important issues of the day. By the election of 1800, this had fundamentally changed the way elections worked. Citizens everywhere were organizing themselves into like-minded groups and consolidating support behind their preferred candidates.[42] That in turn changed how the Electoral College worked. As illustrated by the quote opening this chapter, by 1802—just over a decade after ratification of the original Constitution—presidential electors had begun campaigning for their positions by pledging to cast their votes for the candidates preferred by the people.[43]

The Twelfth Amendment, ratified in 1804, reflected that reality by requiring the electors to cast their votes for president and vice president separately:

> The Electors shall meet in their respective states and vote by ballot for President and Vice-President, one of whom, at least, shall not be an inhabitant of the same state with themselves; they shall name in their ballots the person voted for as President, and in distinct ballots the person voted for as Vice-President, and they shall make distinct lists of all per-

sons voted for as President, and of all persons voted for as Vice-President, and of the number of votes for each, which lists they shall sign and certify, and transmit sealed to the seat of the government of the United States, directed to the President of the Senate.

By designating separate balloting for the offices of president and vice president, the Twelfth Amendment recognized that rather than elite assessments of the character and reputation of individual contenders anticipated by the founders, presidential elections would be structured as competitions among competing political parties representing different ideas and interests. In doing so, the Twelfth Amendment represents a significant shift toward the robust party politics recognizable to us today.

The authors of the Twelfth Amendment considered additional changes as well but ultimately re-adopted most of the rest of the process set out in the 1787 Constitution.[44] Presidents and vice presidents would continue to be elected indirectly through the Electoral College. Electoral votes would continue to be allocated among the states based on each state's congressional delegation, and state legislatures would continue to decide how to appoint their own state's electors. The next big change in the Electoral College process, consequently, came about not because of changes to the Constitution but through changes initiated by elected officials in state legislatures and, ultimately, in Congress. Although these changes were statutory rather than constitutional, they also were triggered by failures of the framers' original compromises over how to elect a president.

———————

The Constitution gives state legislatures the power to determine how their state's electors are chosen. Initially, states used a variety of methods, including direct appointment by the state legislature, statewide popular votes, and district-based popular votes.[45] State legislatures also had no qualms about changing procedures in between presidential elections depending on what method would be more beneficial to the candidate of the party controlling the legislature.[46] But the democratization movement that swept the Jeffersonians into office in 1800 also changed these practices. People expected to be able to vote and they expected their votes to matter. So by the 1830s, almost all states had changed their laws to provide for the popular election of the state's electors.[47] They also, importantly, adopted what is called the general ticket or "unit rule."[48]

The unit rule governs how a state's electoral votes are divided within a state. The 1787 framers probably assumed most states would do this through some sort of districting scheme.[49] In other words, they thought electors would be chosen like members of the House of Representatives are today: by the voters of a particular district within the state, rather than by voters across the state as a whole. Some states did do this at first, but as presidential elections became organized contests between political parties, states shifted to the statewide winner-take-all rules we are familiar with today.[50] In winner-take-all systems, whichever candidate wins a plurality of votes within the state wins all the state's electoral votes. The state's electoral votes, in other words, are cast as a "unit."[51]

Winner-take-all systems maximize a state's influence on the election by awarding 100 percent of a state's electoral votes to a single candidate. One of the first states to switch to the unit system, Virginia, did so for exactly this reason. Virginia switched to the unit rule in 1800 when Jefferson, a Virginian, was running against Adams. By not splitting its votes between the candidates, Virginia made itself more influential in determining the ultimate winner and helped ensure Jefferson's victory.[52]

But the big move to the unit rule came after the 1824 election. Internal divisions and a lack of external competition had split Jefferson's Democratic-Republicans into competing factions, leading to a four-way election between John Quincy Adams (son of John Adams), William Crawford, Henry Clay, and Andrew Jackson.[53] Jackson received the most popular and electoral votes but didn't get a majority of either.[54] Because the Constitution requires a winning candidate to receive a majority, not just a plurality, of electoral votes, the contingent election process was triggered and the election was sent to the House.[55] The House promptly elected John Quincy Adams, infuriating Jackson and his supporters.[56]

Jackson believed the district-based system of choosing electors had contributed to his defeat by enabling too many candidates to pick up stray electoral votes, increasing the chance that even the most popular candidate wouldn't get the constitutionally required majority.[57] The unit rule minimizes that risk by awarding all of a state's electoral votes to the candidate receiving the most votes in that state. So the Jacksonians became vocal supporters of the unit rule.[58] They were effective advocates. By 1836, all states except South Carolina had adopted the unit rule, and it remains the system used in all but two states today.[59] As with the Twelfth Amendment's change to separate balloting for president and vice president, the move to the unit rule has been extremely successful at avoiding the problem it was designed to solve: Since 1824, not a single presidential election has been decided in the House of Representatives under the contingent election process.

Which is not to say there haven't been other issues.

The election of 1844 revealed a problem that will be familiar to American voters today. Whig candidate Henry Clay was in a tight race with Democrat James Polk. James Birney, a third-party candidate running as an abolitionist on the Liberty Party ticket, was also in the race.[60] Birney siphoned off just enough votes from Clay (who was not an abolitionist but was less virulently pro-slavery than Polk) in New York to give Polk a plurality of votes in that state.[61] So New York's Electoral College votes—and therefore the Electoral College victory—went to Polk even though a majority of people even in New York would have undoubtedly preferred Clay over Polk in a two-party race.[62] Birney, in modern lingo, was a spoiler who threw the election to the less popular candidate. Sixteen years later, Abraham Lincoln's victory drew a distinct but related criticism. In 1860, Lincoln won a majority of electoral votes but did so with only a plurality of the nationwide votes, and on purely sectional lines (he received no electoral votes from slaveholding states).[63] To the extent the Electoral College was designed to ensure that a president would have cross-sectional support, Lincoln's election undercut that principle. Unsurprisingly, southern secessionists immediately argued that his election was therefore illegitimate.[64]

But the next Electoral College crisis came after the Civil War, in the 1876 election between Republican Rutherford B. Hayes and Democrat Samuel J. Tilden. The election was held during Reconstruction, the decade after the war when Union troops occupied the south and, to some extent, protected the newly won rights of formerly enslaved Americans to vote and hold office.[65] Tilden (the Democrat) appeared to have won the national popular vote, but who won the Electoral College vote was hotly contested.[66] The war had ended, but northern support for Reconstruction was fraying and white supremacists had been waging a campaign to "redeem" southern states by terrorizing black voters and seizing control of state legislatures through violence and intimidation.[67]

That led to disputes about who controlled the appointment of electors in several of the former Confederate states and whether the reported vote counts were valid. In the resulting confusion, three of those states—Florida, Louisiana, and South Carolina—sent competing slates of electoral votes to Congress.[68] The result was months of conflict and uncertainty, which only ended when southern Democrats agreed to support Hayes in exchange for his promise to end Reconstruction.[69] Hayes became president, but as we will see in Chapter 5 it would be almost one hundred years before Black voting rights were again given meaningful federal protection in the former Confederate states.

These conflicts over competing electoral slates revealed yet another weakness in the Electoral College process. In the 1800 and 1824 elections, everyone had agreed that no candidate had won a majority of electoral votes, and the arguments were about the contingent election in the House. In 1876, in contrast, Congress was confronted with the antecedent question of how to determine which slate of electoral votes received from a state should be accepted as the official votes of the state in the first place. As Congress quickly realized, the constitutional text didn't answer this question. The relevant provision, identical in both the 1787 Constitution and the Twelfth Amendment, reads as follows:

The Electors . . . shall make distinct lists of all persons voted for as President, and all persons voted for as Vice-President and of the number of votes for each, which lists they shall sign and certify, and transmit sealed to the seat of the government of the United States, directed to the President of the Senate; the President of the Senate shall, in the presence of the Senate and House of Representatives, open all the certificates and the votes shall then be counted.

So the president of the Senate (usually the sitting vice president) opens the signed and certified electoral votes, and then they "shall be counted." But what if there is more than one slate of votes, each signed and certified by someone with a plausible claim to speak for the state? The text doesn't contemplate this situation; instead, both the original Constitution and the Twelfth Amendment seem to assume that states will settle disputes about their own slates internally before submitting their electoral votes to Congress. The vicious battles for control of the state governments going on in the 1870s made brutally clear that this would not always be the case; sometimes different factions within a state would send competing slates of electoral votes, each claiming to be the official submission of the state. Plainly, additional changes would be necessary.

———

This time, the changes came from Congress. After the 1876 election, Congress debated the problem at length before eventually enacting the Electoral Count Act of 1887 (ECA).[70] The ECA is not a model of clarity (one of its critical provisions includes a single sentence of 275 words[71]). But the basic framework of the statute is clear. Like the constitutional provisions it derives from, the ECA divides responsibility for presidential elections between the states and Congress, this time by protecting the states' role in resolving their internal election contests while also providing a road map to Congress to guide its actions should a state fail to do so.[72]

The ECA did this by distinguishing between two types of disputes: those about how electors are chosen within a state prior to their appointment (today, the popular vote in the state); and those about how the electors cast their *own* votes after they are appointed (the Electoral College vote). To somewhat oversimplify a complex scheme, the ECA instructed Congress to defer to state determinations about *pre-appointment* disputes as long as the state resolved those disputes by a certain date and through judicial or quasi-judicial contest procedures.[73] But Congress kept for itself the power to resolve *post-appointment* disputes, by authorizing Congress to reject electoral votes that were not "regularly given," such as those cast by people ineligible to be electors (such as federal officers); for a candidate ineligible to be elected (such as a presidential candidate who is not thirty-five years old); or that were cast as the result of an improper influence on the elector (such as if an elector was bribed to vote a particular way).[74]

Additional provisions of federal law applied as well. One section of the ECA established that in certain situations, electoral slates signed by the governor would be treated as presumptively valid.[75] Another established default rules about how members of Congress could object to a state's electoral votes as not "regularly given," and what would happen if the two houses of Congress disagreed about whether a submission met that criterion.[76] A related rule, enacted as part of the Presidential Election Day Act of 1845, allowed state legislatures in states that "failed to make a choice" by the required deadline to appoint electors using procedures other than those established by law prior to election day.[77] The upshot of all of these provisions, though, was that as long as a state followed the statute's procedures and resolved disputes about its own elections in a timely way, Congress would in most cases respect the state's determination.

These rules governed how Congress conducted the electoral count for more than 130 years. But in 2020, defeated candidate Donald J. Trump and a group of his legal advisors insisted that a dizzying array of alternative procedures should govern the process instead. They asserted that uncertified slates of electoral votes submitted by Trump electors in states he lost should be treated as valid competitors to the official state slates;[78] that Congress should independently second-guess state and federal judicial determinations about the fairness of the underlying popular election;[79] and, most shockingly, that the vice president sitting as president of the Senate could unilaterally decide whether to accept or reject a state's official submission.[80] These claims had little legal or factual support and were rejected in state and federal courts across the country.[81] But they did show how the age and complexity of the ECA could enable a losing candidate to distort both the electoral count process and the political discourse surrounding it. So once again Congress responded, this time by enacting the Electoral College Reform Act of 2022 (ECRA).[82] The ECRA, unlike its predecessor, is crisply drafted and relatively straightforward. It clarifies or changes the law in several important ways.

First, it eliminates the "failed to make a choice" provision, replacing it with a more carefully crafted requirement that allows states where elections have been hindered by "extraordinary and catastrophic" conditions to extend or modify voting procedures in accordance with pre-existing state laws.[83] This provision ensures that states that plan ahead and enact appropriate legislation can have procedures in place for extending voting deadlines or modifying other voting procedures during truly catastrophic conditions like terrorist attacks and natural disasters, while avoiding the malleability of the "failed to make a choice" language. It also makes clear that state legislatures cannot in such situations simply sweep in and choose electors themselves. Election procedures can be modified, but a scheduled election cannot be canceled or ignored.[84]

Second, it requires the state governor or other authority designated by state law prior to the election to certify and submit the state's official slate of electoral votes, and to do so using established procedures.[85] It also imposes federal sanctions on state authorities who refuse to follow those procedures when required to do so.[86] Congress in turn is instructed to accept as conclusive electoral votes properly certified and received by the statutory deadline, unless a court orders that the slate be rejected or modified.[87] By clarifying precisely how a slate of electoral votes gains "official" status and requiring Congress to count votes following those procedures, these provisions eliminate the possibility of competing state slates all claiming official status.[88]

Third, the ECRA raises the threshold necessary to trigger a congressional debate about whether to count electoral votes submitted by a state. Under the ECA, an objection was sustained and debated if made in writing and signed by one senator and one member of the House. In recent years, some members of Congress have used the ECA's low threshold for triggering debate to misuse the joint session to vent about the underlying election or to spread election misinformation.[89] The ECRA makes this more difficult by raising the objection threshold to one-fifth of the members of both the House and the Senate.[90]

Finally, the ECRA clarifies the role of the vice president in counting electoral votes. The text of the Constitution says that president of the Senate (usually the sitting vice president) "shall" open the electoral certificates received from the states and that the votes "shall then be counted." Since 1792—more than two hundred years—the actual counting has been done by separate sets of tellers appointed by each house.[91] The vice president has opened the certificates and handed them to the tellers, the tellers count them and report the result to the vice president, and the vice president announces the vote to the chamber.[92] Despite this long-standing practice, Trump claimed after the 2020 election that Vice President Mike Pence could and should unilaterally set aside the electoral votes submitted by several states.[93] The ECRA resoundingly rejects this notion and makes clear that the vice president's role in the joint session is purely ministerial.[94]

In short, the ECRA establishes a clear process to determine which slate of electors is the official slate of a state, makes it a violation of federal law for state officials to refuse to submit those electoral votes, obligates Congress in most situations to accept the states' votes unless a court orders otherwise, significantly raises the threshold necessary for Congress to debate their validity, and clarifies that no single person, including the sitting vice president, gets to pick the next president of the

United States. There are lingering questions about the ability of Congress to bind the actions of state governors and future congresses in these ways,[95] and the ECRA, like the ECA, the Twelfth Amendment, and the original Constitution itself, will not have anticipated every election conflict that could arise or be concocted in the future. Nonetheless, these new provisions make progress toward an Electoral College process that is less subject to future manipulation and better able to facilitate the peaceful transfer of power.

But still. Is there any real reason to continue electing our president this way?

Americans have been asking that question for a very long time. The Electoral College has been the subject of more proposed constitutional amendments—almost eight hundred[96]—than any other part of the Constitution.[97] Many of these proposed amendments passed at least one house of Congress with the required two-thirds majority and several came close to enactment, including efforts in 1950, 1956 and 1969. The 1969 amendment, which would have replaced the Electoral College with a national popular vote, failed in Congress only after being filibustered in the Senate.[98]

Reform efforts are popular with the public. Gallup polling in 1968 reported that an astonishing 81 percent of Americans supported abolishing the Electoral College.[99] In 2000, after Democrat Al Gore become the first candidate in more than one hundred years to win the popular vote but lose the Electoral College (to Republican George W. Bush), two-thirds of Americans, including a roughly equal number of Republicans and Democrats, supported abolishing it.[100] Support among Republican voters dropped after 2016, when another Republican candidate (Trump) won the presidency after losing the popular vote. But even then support remained high and rebounded to 61 percent by 2020 and 65 percent by 2023.[101]

So why does the current system persevere? Part of the problem is simply the difficulty of amending the U.S. Constitution. Amending our

Constitution in most cases requires that a proposed amendment be approved by a two-thirds vote in both houses of Congress.[102] It then further requires legislatures or conventions in three-quarters of the states to approve a proposed amendment.[103] These repeated supermajority requirements have stymied many popular reforms. As in so many other realms of American politics, race discrimination also has played a role. The systemic disenfranchisement of Black Americans after the end of Reconstruction gave white voters in southern states disproportionate power in the Electoral College system, which they would have lost in a national popular vote system.[104] Electoral College reform in the 1960s was regularly filibustered by southern segregationists unwilling to either give up this undeserved advantage or enfranchise Black voters in their states.[105] Civil rights leaders, who understood that the unit rule helped Black voters in northern cities offset Black disenfranchisement in the south, also at times opposed reforms that would take away that option.[106]

Today, though, the biggest barrier to change may be misconceptions about how the current system actually works and, more particularly, who benefits from it. Proponents of keeping the Electoral College tend to rely on three arguments. They argue that the existing system protects the interests of small (low-population) states; that changing the system would lead presidential candidates to ignore most of the country and campaign exclusively in urban centers; and that the Electoral College was intentionally designed by the 1787 framers to be a check on majority power. They also argue that the alternatives would all be worse than the current system.[107]

Each of these claims warrants a closer look.

The argument that small states would suffer if the Electoral College was abolished is probably the one familiar to most people.[108] Historically, though, representatives from small-population states have been as likely as or more likely than their large-state counterparts to support changes to the system.[109] This casts at least some doubt on whether the current scheme is important to the people of those states.[110] More fundamentally, though, small states are not a homogenous bloc and do not seem to have any common interests to protect. According to the 2020 census, the ten states with the smallest populations are Wyoming, Vermont, Alaska, North Dakota, South Dakota, Delaware, Montana, Rhode Island, Maine, and New Hampshire. This is a very diverse group of states. Delaware is the corporate capital of America, Alaska's oil-based economy probably has more in common with Texas than Maine, Rhode Island is the most urbanized state in the nation, and Vermont is the most rural.[111]

These states also have different political leanings. In the 2024 presidential election, they split their votes exactly in half: Five of them cast their electoral ballots for Democrat Kamala Harris (Vermont, Delaware, Rhode Island, Maine,[112] and New Hampshire) while the other five voted for Republican Donald Trump (Wyoming, Alaska, North and South Dakota, and Montana).[113] Moreover, even if these states were politically aligned, the Electoral College system doesn't give them much influence over presidential elections. In 2024, these ten states combined controlled thirty-four electoral votes, just four more than Florida and significantly fewer than either Texas or California.[114] Meaning even if they did vote as a bloc (which they don't), their combined electoral influence would still be relatively small. So protecting the interests of small-population states as such is not a particularly compelling reason to keep the current system.

Which takes us to the second common defense of the Electoral College: Without it, presidential candidates would ignore most of the country and spend their time and money campaigning exclusively in high-population areas, most of which are on the nation's coasts.[115] The problem with this argument is that candidates already ignore most of the country. What drives candidate time and attention today is not whether a state is large or small, rural or urban, or any other demographic dichotomy. Of the ten lowest-population states, nine of them were completely ignored by the 2024 presidential campaigns. The tenth—New Hampshire—enjoyed just two campaign events: one with Harris and one with Trump's running mate, J. D. Vance.[116]

So where are presidential candidates campaigning? In swing states. In 2024, Pennsylvania—the nation's fifth-largest state—was visited a whopping sixty-two times.[117] Michigan and North Carolina were next, followed by Wisconsin and Georgia, then Arizona and Nevada.[118] Of these frequently visited states, only Nevada is even in the lowest third in the nation by population.[119] So whatever small states have to lose by abolishing the Electoral College, it is not candidate time or attention.

A candidate trying to win the national popular vote would certainly spend time campaigning in high-population areas. But they also would be likely to campaign in states with significant political minorities who are ignored under the current system.[120] If every vote mattered as much as every other, Democratic candidates would probably spend more time in Texas and Florida, while Republicans would have more reason to visit Illinois and California. All of these states are currently considered "safe" for one party or the other, but they also are places where *millions* of votes are cast for the minority party. The Electoral College provides little incentive for candidates to mobilize or care about these "submerged minorities," so they are routinely ignored.[121]

That leaves anti-majoritarianism as the final defense of the merits of the current system. The essence of this argument is that we should retain the Electoral College because it was an important part of the 1787 framers' plan to check the power of political majorities.[122] Setting aside whether that alone would be a reason to keep it (the framers both empowered us and expected us to modify their work), this argument misunderstands what the framers thought they were doing when they settled on the Electoral College system. Debates about how to elect the president were focused on parochialism and regionalism, not anti-majoritarianism.[123] The overarching goal of the Electoral College system was not to empower minority vote-winners but to reward consensus candidates (like George Washington) who enjoy broad support across the nation.[124] That is quite different than designing a system for the purpose of electing a candidate who not only lacks that support but is actively opposed by a majority of voters.

The framers were, of course, skeptical of unconstrained majority rule. But as we saw in Chapter 1, they also understood that majority rule was a core component of republican government. So their go-to method of controlling popular sentiment wasn't to empower electoral minorities per se but to channel popular preferences through differently constituted representative institutions.[125] The Electoral College embodies this type of system.[126] In addition to assigning different roles to different institutions, it imposes majoritarian thresholds throughout the process. A successful candidate has to win a majority of electoral votes in order to win the presidency. If no one succeeds in doing so, the election goes to the House, where winning once again requires getting a majority of the votes cast. At each step of this process, the successful candidate must win a majority—not a plurality and certainly not a minority—of the votes cast by similarly situated voters. Nothing in this process was designed to empower minority vote-winners.

To be clear, the 1787 framers didn't expect the winner of the national popular vote to automatically win the presidency. They simply were not thinking in those terms. Their vision of how presidential elections would work was fundamentally different than ours. They assumed states would choose well-respected electors and those electors would exercise their own judgment (via a majority vote) to put the best person in office.[127] Most of the people today defending the anti-majoritarianism of the Electoral College as an important part of the framers' plans are not advocating for a return to that type of system.[128] So they are left defending a system that elevates the preferences of one set of voters, those supporting the popular-vote loser, over the preferences of a group of equally situated voters, their fellow citizens who supported the more popular candidate. Celebrating that outcome is an odd way to honor a system designed to reward candidates who could build consensus support across the nation.

Supporters of the Twelfth Amendment, which modified the original scheme, also were focused on elevating consensus candidates. Unlike the 1787 framers, the men who wrote the Twelfth Amendment were aware of how the original system operated in practice once a uniquely revered figure like George Washington was out of the picture. That knowledge informed how they thought their new system would work. Their expectation, as law professor Ned Foley argues, was not that someone like Washington would emerge very often but rather that winning candidates would achieve broad consensus by winning what Foley calls a "majority of majorities." What he means by that is that they expected a successful candidate to win a popular-vote majority in enough states to then win a majority of the Electoral College.[129] Because of third-party contenders (a thing not anticipated by the authors of the Twelfth Amendment, who were grappling for the first time with the emergence of a two-party system), the system they adopted does not guarantee that a successful candidate will win a majority of the nationwide popular vote. But it does show their efforts to preserve the 1787 framers' goal of rewarding candidates who enjoy broad support across the nation.[130]

If the Electoral College system doesn't protect unique interests shared by low-population states, doesn't incentivize presidential candidates to run truly nationwide campaigns, and wasn't designed by the authors of either the original constitution or the Twelfth Amendment in order to empower minority rule, what, exactly, does it do? Given current demographic, population, and voting trends, it seems to prioritize the political preferences of the older, less racially diverse, and more right-leaning Americans who hold disproportionate voting power in today's battleground states.[131] If there are good reasons to favor the political preferences of these Americans over those of their fellow citizens, supporters of the Electoral College system should make those arguments directly. If not, it may be time to look at the alternatives.

———

Over the decades, different reform movements have focused on different options. One of the earliest was to eliminate winner-take-all unit rules and require states to allocate electors by districts.[132] The 1787 framers probably anticipated that most states would choose their electors through some sort of districting scheme, and a proposed constitutional amendment requiring states to allocate electors that way fell just six House votes short of being approved in 1821.[133] Advocates of eliminating the unit rule and replacing it with an electoral districting scheme argue that districting has some of the same benefits as a national popular vote (i.e., it empowers submerged minorities within the state) without the drawback of requiring a constitutional amendment.[134]

There are practical challenges with this approach, though. Among other things, there is a collective-action problem: A state is unlikely to give up the electoral influence gained by the unit rule unless other states do so as well.[135] But allocating electors by districts has more significant, perhaps fatal, downsides. As virtually all Americans know (and lament), legislative districts can be heavily gerrymandered to advantage the political party drawing the district lines. Today, gerrymanders in some states (most recently, Wisconsin and North Carolina) are so severe that it is difficult for the party out of power to gain a legislative majority even if they win a majority of votes.[136] Using existing congressional districts or districts specially drawn by state legislatures to allocate Electoral College votes would move these pathologies into the presidential election system.

Distributing electoral votes within a state through districting or other types of proportionate schemes creates a second problem as well. By enabling minor-party candidates with geographically concentrated support to win a few electoral votes, it could significantly increase the likelihood that more elections—perhaps most elections—would be decided in the House of the Representatives through the contingent election process. As Andrew Jackson understood, winner-take-all electoral systems prevent this by making it difficult for minor parties to win electoral votes.[137] Eliminating winner-take-all seats in favor of district-based or proportionate allocation of electors could once again permit less-popular candidates to pick up just enough electoral votes to prevent any candidate from getting the constitutionally required majority of electoral votes, triggering the contingent election process.[138] The two-party system may be unpopular, but allowing the House of Representatives to routinely select the president using the one-state/one-vote rule surely is a less palatable alternative. Since the contingent election process cannot be abolished without a constitutional amendment, this nullifies one of the main advantages of these schemes (that they can be accomplished without amending the Constitution).

A more promising option, one that honors voters' interest in supporting minor-party candidates without throwing presidential elections to the House, is to encourage states to adopt ranked-choice or "instant runoff" voting.[139] No less a national figure than James Madison proposed replacing the contingent election process with ranked-choice voting by the electors.[140] Ranked-choice voting systems require voters to rank the competing candidates in order of preference. Candidates with little support are then eliminated and the votes they received are reallocated to their supporters' next preferred choice until someone receives a majority of the votes.[141] Ranked-choice voting, runoff elections (in which a second election is held at a later date between the top finishers if no candidate wins a majority in the first round) and instant runoffs (which do the same thing, but on a single ballot) all share the same objective of ensuring that the final winner is *a* top choice, even if not *the* top choice, of an actual majority of voters.[142]

Ranked-choice voting schemes are popular with voters.[143] They allow voters to avoid having to choose between casting their ballots for the major party candidate most closely aligned with their political preferences or "wasting" their vote on a minor-party candidate whose agenda they more fully support.[144] That same feature also helps minor parties develop and show support, giving them a better chance of emerging over time as viable competitors to the prevailing parties. These voting systems already are used in the United States. Some states, including Maine and Alaska, use ranked-choice voting in both their state and federal elections.[145] Georgia uses a runoff system for statewide races and an instant runoff ballot for overseas and military personnel.[146] If adopted in presidential elections, ranked-choice voting would allow voters to show their support for minor-party candidates without kicking the choice of president to the House of Representatives. It also would do a far better job than the current system of rewarding the type of consensus-building candidates anticipated by the authors of both the 1787 Constitution and the Twelfth Amendment.

Other reform proposals have bounced in and out of the public debate over the years, including keeping the Electoral College system but getting rid of the actual electors by automatically assigning a state's Electoral College vote to the state's popular-vote winner,[147] or doing exactly the opposite by reinvigorating the original framers' idea and permitting electors to vote for whatever candidate they feel is more suitable for the job regardless of the popular vote in their state.[148] Neither of these proposals have gotten much traction, although the first enjoyed some support in the 1960s and the latter was discussed after Trump's unexpected Electoral College victory in 2016.[149] But the most popular alternative today by far is to eliminate the entire Electoral College system and simply elect the president through a national popular vote.[150]

There are various proposals about how to do this. The most well-developed is the National Popular Vote Compact (NPVC), which would formally leave the current system in place but would commit compacting states to cast their state's electoral votes for the national popular-vote winner.[151] The NPVC would go into effect only when joined by enough states so their votes would collectively constitute an Electoral College majority.[152] The point of the compact is to ensure the election of the popular-vote winner without amending the Constitution. So far, seventeen states plus the District of Columbia have signed on, collectively controlling 209 electoral votes. That leaves the compact 61 votes short of the 270 needed to bring it into effect.[153]

The NPVC cleverly leverages the power of state legislatures to decide how their state's electors are chosen. Under the compact, the legislatures of the compacting states make that choice by choosing electors pledged to vote in accordance with the national popular vote, regardless of how the voters in their own state cast their ballots. Unfortunately for supporters of the NPVC, a compact like this among states is of debatable constitutionality.[154] Not because state legislatures acting individually could not choose to appoint electors this way—they probably could—but because the Constitution imposes limits on the extent to which states can agree (compact) with each other to enter into this type of agreement. These limits exist in two provisions of the Constitution, the Treaty Clause and the Compact Clause. The Treaty Clause prohibits any state from entering into "any Treaty, Alliance, or Confederation."[155] The Compact Clause prohibits states from entering into any "agreement or compact" without the consent of Congress.[156] The exact meaning of these clauses is historically opaque and judicially underdeveloped (there are no Supreme Court cases clearly defining what they mean), but it is clear that Congress must approve at least some agreements between the states.[157] That means any effort to enforce the compact would be immediately challenged in court and might well be struck down as unconstitutional.[158]

Even beyond this constitutional uncertainty, though, there are other difficulties with the NPVC. It is unclear if the compact, even if approved by Congress, could be enforced in the critical months immediately preceding a presidential election. Because the Constitution gives state legislatures the power to choose how their state's electors are chosen, even those states that have entered into the compact may have a constitutional right to leave the compact before any particular election. The NPVC attempts to mitigate this risk by limiting the conditions under which states can exit the agreement, but it is far from clear whether or how those provisions would be enforced.[159] Opponents of the compact also argue that it is unconstitutional for state legislatures to hold a popular vote in their state but ignore the results of that vote when appointing the state's electors.[160] Like the application of the Compact Clause to the NPVC, courts have not yet fully engaged these questions. All of this means that the NPVC, even if adopted by enough states, would almost certainly be tied up in court for years and may never be implemented.

In the end, then, the most straightforward solution to our Electoral College problem may also be the most difficult: Amend the Constitution and elect the president through a national popular vote. Especially if combined with a ranked-choice or instant runoff system, a national popular vote would almost certainly do a better job than the current system in honoring the intentions of the authors of the 1787 Constitution and the Twelfth Amendment to reward consensus candidates.

This solution, though, raises a new objection. Choosing the president through a national popular vote would almost certainly lead to pressure on Congress to create more uniformity in voting practices and procedures across the country by enacting new federal election laws.[161] There already is a great deal of similarity in how voters across the nation cast their votes, but states retain some important areas of autonomy over how their elections operate, which means voters in different states often vote in different ways. Those differences could easily create a perception of unfairness in a national popular vote system, where all votes are pooled together to determine the winner. That, in turn, would sharpen existing questions about the division of power between Congress and the states about who makes the rules governing our elections, which is what we will turn to next.

Four

Making the Rules

> The question here is whether tens of thousands of Wisconsin citizens can vote safely in the midst of a pandemic. . . . Either they will have to brave the polls, endangering their own and others' safety. Or they will lose their right to vote, through no fault of their own. That is a matter of utmost importance—to the constitutional rights of Wisconsin's citizens, the integrity of the State's election process, and in this most extraordinary time, the health of the Nation.
>
> —JUSTICE RUTH BADER GINSBURG,
> dissenting, 2020[1]

People who lived through the spring of 2020 are unlikely to forget it. News of a new virus emerged out of China and spread across the globe. Much about the virus and its associated illness, which we would come to call Covid-19, was unknown, including how it was transmitted and how fatal it was. There was no vaccine, and there were few widely available treatments for those who became seriously ill. Public health officials were scrambling to find answers.

Covid-19 also caused problems for election administrators, who were struggling with a problem of their own: how to conduct an election in the midst of a global pandemic. It was a presidential election year, and several states, including political bellwethers like Wisconsin and Ohio, had important spring primaries coming up. Election officials worried about how to ensure the safety of both voters and poll workers, especially in those early days when so much about the virus was unknown.

This extraordinary situation set the stage for what became some of the most intensely fought battles of the 2020 election. In a flurry of activity, governors, secretaries of state, state legislatures, and local election boards adopted an array of rules and policies governing how people would cast their votes in the upcoming elections. Most of their solutions were not new. States had been allowing voters to do things like register online and vote by mail for decades.[2] But the pandemic expanded their reach, and the politics of 2020 put them under a magnifying glass. Many voters encountered these alternative voting methods for the first time when they cast their own ballots. Others were primed to be suspicious of them when used by voters in other states. All of which left many Americans wondering what the rules governing our elections are, and who gets to make them.

This chapter tackles that question. It begins by looking at the choices made in 1787 about how to divide authority over elections between Congress and the state legislatures. It then examines how that original division of authority underlies disputes today about hot-button issues such as preventing noncitizens from voting, combating partisan gerrymandering, and constraining the role of state legislatures in picking the president. As we will see, two little-known provisions of the 1787 Constitution have had a big impact on who makes the rules about how our elections work.

———

The United States does not really have one election system; we have thousands. States, cities, and counties adopt different procedures governing their elections. That can create confusion, as it did in 2020, when people suddenly realized that not all voters follow the same rules. It can feel unfair, or even suspect. But like so many things in our system, authority over elections is constitutionally divided, this time between the states and the federal government. That means election rules can and do vary, even when the election is for a national office like the presidency.

There are limits to this variety, of course. The Fifteenth, Nineteenth, and Twenty-sixth Amendments prohibit discrimination in voting on the basis of race, sex, and age, and the Fourteenth Amendment limits the ability of states to impose certain burdens on the right to vote. Congress also has power to enact federal laws enforcing these prohibitions. We discuss those issues in the next chapter. This chapter addresses two different constitutional provisions: The Qualifications and Elections Clauses of Article 1 of the Constitution. These clauses are probably unfamiliar to most Americans today, but together they structure the basic division of power between states and the federal government in regard to federal elections. In 1787, they also they were among the most controversial provisions of the proposed constitution drafted in Philadelphia.

As we saw in Chapter 2, delegates at the Constitutional Convention quickly agreed that members of the House of Representatives would be elected by the people, but there was much less agreement about who would make the rules governing those elections. The states had been regulating their own elections for decades, going back to the earliest colonial assemblies. Unsurprisingly, they all had different rules, including rules about who was eligible to vote. No state let everyone vote. In addition to age, race, and gender restrictions, many states also limited the franchise to property owners.[3] These property requirements varied across the states. Some states allowed the payment of a tax or ownership of other forms of property (other than land) to count, but many didn't.[4] The states that imposed these limitations also varied significantly in how much property a man had to hold, or how much tax he had to pay, in order to be eligible.[5]

This created a dilemma for the drafters of the 1787 Constitution. Delegates at the Constitutional Convention were themselves fairly wealthy, and many of them believed that economic independence of the sort they personally enjoyed was essential for the responsible exercise of the franchise.[6] They also were leery of giving state legislatures, which they generally viewed as corrupt, unlimited control over federal elections.[7] All of which led many of the 1787 framers to want to decide for themselves who would be eligible to vote in federal elections, rather than leaving that task to the states.

But they were unsure what restrictions on the franchise (the right to vote) they should impose. White men in the south were generally much wealthier than their northern counterparts, so a dollar amount that would be appropriately exclusionary (in their view) in the south would be devastatingly broad in the north.[8] Likewise, any federal property qualification other than the most lenient would disenfranchise existing voters in states with lower qualifications.[9] Men accustomed to voting in their state elections would be unlikely to support ratification of a new constitution that would deprive them of the vote in future federal elections.[10] Because the new constitution would be ratified in each state by special delegates elected by the voters of each state, the drafters knew this could seriously undermine the success of the entire project.[11]

Their solution was clever. Rather than create a single federal qualification, the 1787 framers let the states define voter qualifications for federal elections, but they also required that those qualifications be the same ones the state used to define eligibility to vote for members of the most numerous branch of the state legislature (usually the state assembly). The idea was that state legislators would be less likely to manipulate the federal franchise if doing so would affect their own elections as well. The language accomplishing this is the Qualifications Clause, found in Article I, Section 2:

> The House of Representatives shall be composed of Members chosen every second Year by the People of the several States, and the Electors in each State shall have the Qualifications requisite for Electors of the most numerous Branch of the State Legislature.[12]

This solution allowed the framers to avoid coming up with a single rule for the entire nation. But it didn't fully resolve their concerns about state manipulation of federal elections. They also were concerned that hostile state legislatures might kneecap the federal government by refusing to hold federal elections at all, preventing the House of Representatives—and therefore Congress—from functioning.[13] Their solution to that problem was to give initial responsibility for regulating federal elections to the states but to allow Congress to supersede those regulations when it saw fit. Specifically, Congress was given power to override state choices regarding the "times, places, and manner" of holding elections for Congress, excepting only the "places" of choosing the state's U.S. senators.[14]

Article I, Section 4, the Elections Clause, sets this out:

> The Times, Places and Manner of holding Elections for Senators and Representatives, shall be prescribed in each State by the Legislature thereof; but the Congress may at any time by Law make or alter such Regulations, except as to the Places of chusing Senators.

These two clauses—the Elections Clause and the Qualifications Clause—work together to form the original division of authority over federal elections. They don't govern all issues arising in this area, as we'll see in the next chapter. Congress has power to regulate many aspects of both state and federal elections under other constitutional provisions, but they are a good starting point in figuring out who makes the rules about how our elections work.

Three things about these clauses warrant immediate attention.

First, neither Congress nor the states can use their Elections or Qualifications powers to violate other parts of the Constitution. So for example, the Twenty-fourth Amendment prohibits states from imposing a poll tax as a voting qualification in federal elections, and a decision of the U.S. Supreme Court prohibits such taxes in regard to voting in state elections.[15] Nothing in the Elections or Qualifications Clauses give states or Congress authority to ignore constitutional requirements like these. The Constitution imposes several limitations like this, many of which we'll discuss in the next chapter.

Second, both the Elections and Qualifications Clauses only apply to federal elections. Think about how our elections work. When you go to vote, you usually vote for state and federal candidates on the same ballot. During a presidential year, you might vote for a president, a member of the House of Representatives, a state senator, the governor of your state, and maybe a member of your local county board or city commission. Only two of these positions are federal offices. Yet you almost certainly cast your votes for all of these offices in the same way and using the same procedures, even though Congress only has power under the Elections Clause to override state choices about federal elections. There are both practical and legal reasons for this. Practically, states for the most part (we'll discuss some exceptions below) have been unwilling to have separate election rules for state and federal elections, so the rules Congress makes under the Elections Clause tend to be adopted by states for state and local elections as well. In addition, legally, the constitutional amendments adopted after the Civil War gave Congress additional power to make election rules governing both federal and state elections. As we will see in the next chapter, that also generates quite a bit of uniformity across state and federal elections, although meaningful differences among the states do still exist.

Finally, the Elections and Qualifications Clauses differ as to who between Congress and the states gets the final word on different types of election rules. The Qualifications Clause gives the final say about voter qualifications to the states, as long as those choices don't violate other parts of the Constitution. But the Elections Clause allows Congress power to override state choices about the "times, places, and manner" of federal elections. This makes the distinction between a voter qualification and a time, place, and manner regulation an important one. Under Article I, Congress can't change a state's choices about voter qualifications, but it can override state rules about the times, places and manner of holding federal elections.[16]

This division of authority, especially the times, places, and manner provision of the Elections Clause, gives Congress significant authority to make the rules governing elections. Giving such vast power to Congress was controversial. Opponents of the 1787 Constitution tried to restrict or eliminate the times, places, and manner provision before the Constitution was ratified.[17] Patrick Henry, then a member of the Virginia state legislature and an opponent of ratification, was afraid Congress would use the power to make it difficult for voters to participate in federal elections by forcing states to hold votes in remote parts of the states (something the British had done before the revolution).[18] "Cato," the pseudonym used by another influential opponent of ratification, thought Congress could use its times, places and manner power to control who was elected to Congress.[19] Delegates at the Massachusetts ratifying convention went even further, arguing that members of Congress could use it to perpetuate their own power by completely eliminating federal elections.[20]

Supporters of the 1787 Constitution dismissed some of these concerns as farfetched, but they also defended the breadth of congressional power on the merits. A federal government, they argued, had to have final authority over federal elections or else the states would be able to use their power over elections to weaken the new national government. In the ratification debates in Pennsylvania, James Wilson argued that the provision was essential to "the very existence of the federal government."[21] Pro-ratification delegate Rufus King, from Massachusetts, said the times, places, and manner provision was necessary to prevent rogue states from refusing to hold federal elections at all.[22] Even Alexander Hamilton chimed in. "I am greatly mistaken," he wrote in Federalist 59, "if there be any article in the whole plan more completely defensible than this."[23] The propriety of the provision, he argued, rested on the "plain proposition" that every government needs to be able to ensure its own preservation.[24]

In the end, the Elections Clause and the Qualifications Clause both survived. Under these provisions, Congress cannot interfere with a state legislature's choice about the qualifications of the state's voters, but it does have the final say over rules regulating the times, places, and manner of federal elections.[25] Understanding how these clauses shape our current controversies requires us to go back to 2012 and take a look at a U.S. Supreme Court case called *Arizona v. Inter Tribal Council of Arizona*.[26]

Inter Tribal involved the National Voter Registration Act (NVRA), enacted in 1993. Among other things, the NVRA created a standardized, nationwide process that voters can use to submit their voter registration forms by mail.[27] The NVRA allows voters across the country to register to vote by completing a particular form, called the federal form, and sending it to whoever in their state is charged with processing voter registrations.[28] The NVRA requires all states to accept this form when registering voters for federal elections.

The dispute in *Inter Tribal* arose because Arizona was unsatisfied with the way the federal form allowed registrants to prove they were U.S. citizens. There is little evidence that noncitizen voting is a problem in our elections, and it was (and remains) illegal under both federal and Arizona state law.[29] The dispute in *Inter Tribal* wasn't about that prohibition itself but rather about how a prospective voter verifies their citizenship. How to best do this is a subject of active debate, but at the time of *Inter Tribal*, federal law did so by requiring registrants using the federal form to check a box on the form attesting under penalty of perjury and deportation that they are U.S. citizens, and requiring states to cross-check registration information with other datasets.[30] Arizona thought this was insufficient and wanted to require applicants to provide documentary proof of citizenship (such as a birth certificate or passport) before they were allowed to register.[31]

So the Arizona state legislature passed a state law requiring registrants to include copies of that type of documentation when submitting their registration forms.[32] This created a potential conflict between the federal and state laws. The federal law required states to "accept and use" the federal registration form, which allowed registrants to attest to their citizenship status by checking the applicable box. Arizona's law said that wasn't good enough and required registrants to also provide documentary proof of citizenship. In our constitutional system, a valid federal law supersedes (or "preempts") a conflicting state law. That means that as long as Congress had constitutional authority to enact the NVRA, the federal law would preempt Arizona's law and Arizona would have to allow voters to register using the federal form.[33]

Much of *Inter Tribal* is about whether the two laws actually created a conflict, but the case also raised a question about Congress's power under the Elections and Qualifications Clauses. If requiring states to use the federal form was the regulation of the times, places, or manner of holding federal elections, Congress could override Arizona's choice under the Elections Clause. But if it involved a voter qualification under the Qualifications Clause, Arizona would get the final word.

So which was it?

The answer is that the dispute is about a times, places, or manner regulation, not a voter qualification. Why? Because Congress and Arizona *agree* that U.S. citizenship is a necessary qualification for voting in federal elections. That's not what they are arguing about. Rather they are arguing about how a registrant proves they are a citizen. Congress says they can do so by attestation under penalty of perjury on the federal form, while Arizona wants documentary evidence. That is not a dispute about the qualification itself, it's a dispute over the manner in which the qualification is demonstrated.

Justice Antonin Scalia wrote the decision for the Court. He first underscored the sweeping scope of congressional power under the Elections Clause. The Supreme Court, Scalia wrote, has repeatedly held that "times, places, and manner" are "comprehensive words" that "embrace authority to provide a complete code for congressional elections," including how to register voters.[34] Rules about how a voter demonstrates their citizenship are within the scope of that power, Scalia wrote.[35] So *Inter Tribal* makes clear that Congress's Elections Clause power is and remains broad. But Scalia went on to point out that the interplay between the Elections and Qualifications Clauses does impose some restrictions on how Congress uses that power. Specifically, he wrote, Congress cannot use its Elections Clause power in a way that negates the ability of the states to enforce their chosen voter qualifications.[36]

This is a common form of constitutional argument. Even when the

Constitution clearly grants power to a particular official or governmental branch to do something, that entity can't use that power to nullify the ability of a different part of government to exercise its own constitutionally granted powers. So, for example, Congress unequivocally has the power to determine how to spend federal revenues—it writes the budget. But it can't use that power to completely defund the executive branch, because doing so would leave presidents unable to exercise the power the Constitution gives them to fulfill the duties of their office.

Arizona argued that this is exactly what the federal law did by forcing it to accept the attestation of citizenship used on the federal form.[37] By prohibiting the state from also requiring documentary proof of citizenship at the time of registration, Arizona argued that it was unable to enforce its citizenship qualification, which it was constitutionally entitled to do.[38] Justice Scalia was sympathetic to this argument but pointed out that it had not been adequately raised or developed in the case before the Court.[39] A lower federal court heard arguments on that issue in a subsequent case, but found that Arizona failed to show that using the federal form precluded it from obtaining the information necessary to enforce its qualification.[40]

So Arizona lost the battle, but concerns about noncitizen voting have not abated and Arizona has not given up. Instead, Arizona has opted to use a two-tiered registration system.[41] Voters showing documentary proof of citizenship can be registered to vote in both state and federal elections using a state form, but those using the federal form attesting to citizenship are registered as "federal only" voters and are not permitted to vote in state or local elections unless other documentary proof of citizenship is available.[42] That makes Arizona one of only a handful of states since passage of the Voting Rights Act who have tried to operate separate registration systems in order to avoid election regulations enacted by Congress.[43] Its choice to do so remains controversial and continues to be challenged by voting rights groups, but the Supreme Court has not yet revisited the issue.[44]

The Supreme Court has, however, jumped into a related dispute: What does it mean to give power to regulate federal elections to the "legislature" of each state? The Elections Clause says that the times, places, and manner of holding elections for federal officers shall, at least as an initial matter, be prescribed in each state "by the legislature thereof." Its twin provision, the Electors Clause that we looked at in the last chapter, uses the same language to describe how states choose their presidential electors.[45] The legal question presented in both of these clauses is what it means to assign that task to "the legislature" of each state.

After the 2020 election, some of Donald Trump's supporters latched onto the term "legislature" to argue that state legislatures had virtually unlimited power to choose the state's presidential electors, even after election day and even in ways that violated state law.[46] These clauses, they argued, give authority over federal elections to "the legislature" of each state and, therefore, no other state entity can constrain how the state legislature uses that power. The state legislature is "independent" of state laws that would otherwise limit its authority.

The Supreme Court had briefly addressed this argument twenty years earlier, in *Bush v. Gore*.[47] In that case, also decided in the midst of a contested presidential election, three members of the Court wrote a separate opinion saying that the Florida Supreme Court had interpreted Florida state law so badly that it was no longer acting as a court and had violated the "legislature thereof" language of the Electors Clause by intruding on the Florida state legislature's power to make Florida's election laws.[48] In 2020, Trump's supporters argued that the pandemic-era voting rules made by governors, secretaries of state, and other state and local officials had done the same thing.[49] After Trump lost that election, some of his supporters went even further, arguing that the Electors Clause entitled state legislatures to ignore the election results in their state and give their state's electoral votes to whichever candidate the state legislature chose.[50]

The scope of those arguments was unprecedented—even the three-justice concurrence in *Bush v. Gore* had not gone that far—and got no sympathy from the courts.[51] But a similar argument, involving the "legislature thereof" language in the Elections Clause, had been working its way through the courts for years. The Supreme Court addressed this version of the argument in *Arizona Legislature v. Arizona Independent Redistricting Commission*[52] and *Moore v. Harper*.[53] Both of these cases involved "partisan gerrymandering," the drawing of legislative district lines to benefit the line-drawer's political party.

To the dismay of many Americans, in 2019 the Supreme Court had decided in *Rucho v. Common Clause* that partisan gerrymandering was "nonjusticiable" under the U.S. Constitution.[54] "Nonjusticiability" is a judicial doctrine holding that even though a challenged practice may in some sense violate the Constitution, it isn't the job of the federal courts to invalidate it, usually because the Constitution gives responsibility over the dispute to a different branch of government or because the topic doesn't lend itself to legal resolution.[55] Very few issues are nonjusticiable, but after a decade of debate the Court decided in *Rucho* that partisan gerrymandering was one of them. That means federal courts will not strike down partisan gerrymanders as unconstitutional, no matter how egregious.

But nothing in *Rucho* prohibited state supreme courts from deciding whether partisan gerrymandering violated state constitutions. State supreme courts usually have final say over the meaning of state laws, including state constitutions. The role of federal judges in such cases is not to decide for themselves what state law means but to determine whether the state law as interpreted by the state supreme court conflicts with any federal law or the federal Constitution. If so, the state law is preempted and invalid. If not, the state court's interpretation of its own state's law stands, even if the federal court thinks the state's interpretation of the law is wrong. This relationship between state and federal courts is a core component of our federalist system and ensures that states get to decide what their own laws mean, using their own history, precedents, and practices.[56] *Arizona Independent Redistricting Commission* and *Moore* are about whether the Elections Clause limits a state court's power to do that when interpreting state laws regulating federal elections.

Arizona Independent Redistricting Commission came first. It arose when the people of Arizona, frustrated by aggressive gerrymanders in their state, used a ballot initiative to take districting out of the hands of the state legislature and give it to an independent redistricting commission.[57] Ballot initiatives are a form of direct lawmaking. The process varies from state to state, and not all states permit them, but generally speaking ballot initiatives are a way to let citizens engage in direct democracy by voting on issues directly.[58] The Arizona Constitution permits the use of ballot initiatives to make binding state laws, and even to change the state constitution.[59] The people of Arizona used that process to bypass the state legislature and enact the law creating the independent districting commission.

The Arizona state legislature didn't like that and sued. It claimed that using the ballot initiative process to change the state's districting process violated the Elections Clause because laws made through ballot initiatives are not made by "the legislature" of the state. Therefore, it argued, using that process to change the state's districting process conflicted with the federal Constitution and was unconstitutional, at least as applied to the state's congressional (federal) districts. So the question presented in the Arizona redistricting commission case was what, for purposes of the Elections Clause, is the state legislature?

This may seem like an easy question: The legislature is the legislature. But state legislatures are creations of state constitutions, and those constitutions impose rules on how they make laws.[60] For example, all but one state (Nebraska) has a bicameral legislature, and the constitutions of those states make clear that the law-making process of the state requires both houses of the legislature to concur before a bill becomes a law. State constitutions also give governors power to veto state laws and state supreme courts power to interpret them. So the issue in *Arizona Independent Redistricting Commission* was not really as simple as "is the legislature the legislature," but whether the Elections Clause intended to override all these other rules about how states make their laws. In other words, does the Elections Clause necessarily refer exclusively to a state's legislative body, or does it also include the overall lawmaking process as adopted by a state in its own state constitution?

The Supreme Court, siding with the Arizona voters, opted for the latter reading.[61] Justice Ruth Bader Ginsburg wrote the majority opinion. For purposes of the Elections Clause, she wrote, "the legislature" included not just the formal legislative body but also any lawmaking process authorized by state law.[62] Because the Arizona state constitution authorized the use of ballot initiatives to make state law, that process was part of the state's lawmaking process and could be used to make laws regulating the state's congressional elections.[63] One of the basic functions of a state constitution, Ginsburg wrote, is to create the state government and define the powers of its different branches.[64] This includes defining the steps necessary to make state law, which in Arizona included making laws through ballot initiatives.

Once again, the Court reached back to 1787 to defend its decision. Nothing in the history of the Elections Clause, Ginsburg wrote, indicated that the authors of the original Constitution intended that clause to supersede a state's normal lawmaking procedures.[65] Doing so would have been a major intrusion by the federal government into how states govern their own internal affairs. Given how controversial it was for the Constitution to give Congress the override power in the first place, it would have been truly exceptional for that same provision to have invaded state autonomy even further by dictating to states how they could and could not make their own laws.[66] Surely, Ginsburg argued, if the clause had been intended to make that big a change to the states' internal procedures, someone would have mentioned it during the ratification debates.[67] But nobody did.[68]

Ginsburg also pointed out some of the striking consequences of the Arizona legislature's reasoning. If "the legislature" means exclusively the institutional legislature, she noted, then a state governor would be unable to veto any legislation regulating federal elections because the governor is not part of the institutional legislature.[69] State courts likewise would be barred from issuing binding decisions about the meanings of state laws regulating federal elections, because they aren't "the legislature" either.[70] Ginsburg's point is that the authors of the 1787 Constitution surely would not have used a vehicle like the Elections Clause to make such sweeping changes to the lawmaking procedures already in places in states across the nation. Any effort to do so would have generated vehement opposition at the ratifying conventions, rather than the utter silence on the point revealed by the historical record. Consequently, to the majority, nothing in the Elections Clause barred Arizona citizens from using the ballot initiative process authorized by the Arizona state constitution to enact Arizona's laws governing federal elections, including laws restricting partisan gerrymandering.

Chief Justice John Roberts wrote the main dissent. The term used in the Elections Clause, he wrote, is "legislature," not "lawmaking process."[71] The term "state legislature" is used many times in the Constitution, he argued, and always to refer to the elected body that holds legislative power in the state.[72] Attributing a different meaning to the term in just this one provision of the federal constitution is contrary to the normal judicial practice of presuming the same word means the same thing when used in the same document.[73] To Roberts, that didn't mean the state could never authorize alternative lawmaking procedures, or entirely ignore its normal lawmaking procedures, but it did mean that the institutional legislature could not be cut out of the lawmaking process entirely.[74] Because the ballot initiative process used in Arizona did not give the legislature *any* role in enacting the law creating the independent districting commission, it didn't pass the minimum requirements of the Elections Clause and was, in his view, unconstitutional.[75]

————

Justice Ginsburg's reasoning carried the day in *Arizona Independent Districting Commission*, but the Court looked very different when the issue came back to it in 2023, in *Moore v. Harper*.[76] Ginsburg had died three years earlier, and four new justices, three of whom were appointed by Trump, were now sitting on the Supreme Court.[77] So when the Court agreed to revisit the "legislature thereof" issue in *Moore v. Harper*, it looked like Chief Justice Roberts might have the final say after all.

Like *Arizona Independent Districting Commission*, *Moore* involved partisan gerrymandering, this time in North Carolina. The law challenged in *Moore* was a North Carolina congressional districting scheme designed by the state's majority-Republican legislature to create as many Republican districts as possible.[78] Under the districting plan, ten of the state's fourteen congressional districts were likely to fall under Republican control, despite the much more evenly divided partisan split of the state's voters.[79] A group of North Carolina voters challenged the plan, arguing that it violated several provisions of the state constitution, including one guaranteeing "free elections."[80] The North Carolina Supreme Court agreed and threw out the plan, holding that extreme partisan gerrymanders violated the state constitution.[81]

Echoing the arguments rejected by the Court in *Arizona Independent Districting Commission*, the challengers in *Moore* insisted that the state supreme court could have no role in defining the state's election laws because the Elections Clause gave that job exclusively to the state legislature.[82] Specifically, Moore, the Republican leader of the North Carolina House of Representatives, argued that the state legislature had a federal constitutional right to create the state's election laws unbound by state law restrictions, including those imposed by the state constitution. In other words, Moore argued that the Elections Clause gave the state legislature a right to violate its own state constitution, as interpreted by its own state supreme court, when regulating federal (but not state) elections. This is the essence of the "independent state legislature" theory: When making rules regulating federal elections, state legislatures are "independent" of the rules that normally constrain them.[83]

Chief Justice Roberts wrote the majority opinion. But instead of expanding on his *Arizona Independent Districting Commission* dissent, he rejected Moore's argument.[84] Writing for himself and five other justices, Roberts affirmed that nothing in the history of the Elections Clause, the practices of state and federal courts, or the U.S. Supreme Court's own precedents supported Moore's expansive interpretation of the Elections Clause.[85] The clause, Roberts concluded, "does not insulate state legislatures from the ordinary exercise of state judicial review."[86]

Like the three-justice opinion in *Bush v. Gore*, Roberts left open the possibility that a state supreme court decision going too far beyond the "ordinary bounds" of judicial review could violate the federal Constitution by intruding on power reserved by the Elections Clause to the state legislatures, but the parties had not argued that that had happened in the case presented.[87] That caveat does leave some wiggle room for federal courts to rein in state supreme court decisions they see as egregiously wrong, but it appears (for now) that as long as state court judges use standard tools of legal reasoning when reviewing state laws governing federal elections, their decisions about the meaning of those laws will be final and binding on state legislatures, including state court decisions involving partisan gerrymandering.[88]

So where does this leave us in our understanding of who makes the rules governing our elections? As we've seen, the Elections and Qualifications Clauses are yet another part of our constitutional system where governing power is divided between one or more entities, in this case between Congress and the state legislatures. State legislatures make the initial rules regulating our elections, but Congress has broad authority to override those rules for federal elections. States get the final say over the qualifications of their voters (subject to other constitutional constraints), and Congress can't use its override power to unconstitutionally hinder their ability to impose those qualifications. But state legislatures do have to abide by restrictions imposed by their state's own laws and state constitutions when making election rules for their state, including rules governing federal elections.

With this understanding of who makes the rules, we are now ready to take a closer look at just what those rules are. With so many Americans expressing uncertainty about the integrity of our elections, it is important for all of us to better understand how they actually work. The remainder of this chapter will focus on that issue.

————

As we've seen, election rules can vary from one state to another, and even from one jurisdiction to another within the same state. Most jurisdictions, though, follow similar basic procedures regarding how voters register and cast their ballots and how those ballots are counted and (sometimes) contested. These basic procedures are outlined in this section. This is not a comprehensive survey of the law in every state, but it is a description of the sort of procedures that states routinely follow.

If you are reading this book you are probably a voter, so many of these procedures will be familiar to you. The first step in voting is to register. How far in advance you had to complete your registration will depend on your state. About a third of the states permit residents to register and vote on the same day, meaning voters don't have to plan very far ahead in order to vote; others require voters to register as early as a month before election day.[89] Most states also allow voters to complete the registration process online, but a few require registrants to fill out and return a printed form.[90] Whether registering online or in person, registrants in all states must provide identifying information, such as a social security or driver's license number, when they register.[91] In addition, states that hold "closed" partisan primary elections ask registrants to identify their political party, to ensure that only members of that party vote in their party's primary.[92] Those with open or nonpartisan primaries need not collect this information.

States don't have unlimited discretion over how they design their voter registration systems; as we saw earlier, some federal laws apply. The most important of these are NVRA (discussed previously) and the Help America Vote Act (HAVA). NVRA requires all states to offer residents the opportunity to register when they interact with certain state and local governmental offices.[93] This includes the state's department of motor vehicles, which is where the law's nickname—the "Motor Voter Law"—comes from. NVRA also requires states to offer voters the option of registering by mail.[94]

HAVA, passed by Congress in 2002, also addresses registration. Under HAVA, states must require new voters who register by mail to confirm their identity. Voters can do this either by providing identification numbers that can be cross-checked with state databases or by showing certain forms of identification the first time they vote.[95] Acceptable forms of identification under HAVA include a current and valid photo ID, a copy of a utility bill, a paycheck, or another form of government document showing the registrant's current address.[96] Most states also require even longtime voters to show identification at the polls, but HAVA itself does not impose this requirement on all voters, only those who register by mail and only the first time they vote.[97]

These laws also constrain how states manage their voter rolls. Voter rolls are the large datasets maintained by states that keep track of who is registered to vote in their state. People move, die, and change their residency all the time, which can make this challenging. So federal law requires states to work to ensure the accuracy of their rolls by checking them against other large datasets, such as department of motor vehicle and social security records, state and federal criminal conviction records, and USPS change-of-address information.[98] But the law also protects voters by restricting when and how they can be dropped from the rolls.[99] By requiring voter rolls to be updated regularly following procedures set out in advance in state and federal law, these requirements strike a balance between requiring states to maintain up-to-date voter registration information and eliminating undue burdens on voters. It also minimizes the inevitable human errors that would result from requiring voters to re-register for every election. This system avoids mistakenly disenfranchising eligible voters but does mean that at any given moment the rolls will include some inaccuracies. That isn't evidence of a problem; it's just what happens when rolls are updated in a systemic way on regularized schedules.[100]

Once voters are registered, states remain free, within broad param-eters, to determine for themselves how their residents actually cast their ballots. Even before the 2020 pandemic, states had adopted an array of different voting methods to make voting easier. Most states (before 2020, all but seven) had "no-excuse absentee voting," which allows voters to vote by mail without showing that they have a special need to do so.[101] Five states, including reliably blue Oregon and deep red Utah, have used predominantly mail-in systems for decades.[102] These states usually im-plement these systems by automatically mailing ballots to all active reg-istered voters (voters who both are registered and have voted in recent elections) as part of their regular pre-election process.[103] States also have for decades done things like permit voters to request and receive ballots by mail, drop off completed ballots in person or in designated reposi-tories, and allow individuals or groups to collect and return completed ballots on behalf of voters.[104]

All states also include as part of their regular procedures multiple and redundant election security measures. From the time ballots are or-dered, election officials carefully track all of them. Ballots are regularly counted and recounted.[105] Election officials know how many ballots they have received, where they have sent them, and whether they have been returned.[106] All registered voters are assigned a unique voter identifica-tion number.[107] When a voter requests a ballot by mail, that number is usually printed on the envelope the voter uses to return their ballot (to ensure voter privacy, it is separated from the ballot itself before the vote is counted).[108] When a voter votes in person, the voter roll is marked to show that the person associated with that number has voted.[109]

These procedures help ensure that only one ballot is cast per voter. If a voter shows up at their polling place to try to vote a second time, or requests an absentee ballot after already voting or returning one, the system will show that the person associated with that voter number has already cast their ballot.[110] These unique identification numbers also enable voters in some states to track the progress of their vote online and confirm that it has been counted.[111] (If you live in a state that allows you to electronically track your ballot, you can probably see your unique voter identification number by logging into your voter account.)

There are additional security checks in places during voting itself. Photo or other forms of identification, signature matches, or both are required and verified when voters check in at their polling places.[112] Many voters physically sign a poll book before they vote.[113] States also require mailed-in ballot materials to include voter signatures, which are checked, often in addition to other identification numbers, when these ballots are opened and separated to be counted.[114] Voting machines, including the equipment used to count votes, must be stored in secure locations with limited and controlled access.[115] This equipment is regularly tested, and the U.S. Election Assistance Commission's testing and certification program prohibits this equipment from connecting wirelessly to external networks.[116] In addition, paper verification procedures in most states allow in-person voters to confirm that their vote was properly captured by viewing a physical record of their vote before leaving their polling places.[117] Those paper verifications are then used to audit the machine tallies of electronically cast votes.[118]

After all the votes are cast, they must be counted. There also are extensive regulations regarding how this is done. In most states, local elections boards oversee the initial vote count.[119] In smaller jurisdictions, ballots often are counted in the precinct where they are cast.[120] Larger jurisdictions are more likely to use central counting facilities, which can more efficiently process large numbers of ballots.[121] No state releases results before polls close in the state, but states do have different rules governing when election officials can begin processing and counting ballots, which can slow down results in states prohibiting any sort of pre-processing.[122] States also routinely conduct a post-balloting canvass to reconcile the number of ballots cast with the number of people who voted, resolve issues regarding provisional ballots and ballot-marking errors, and verify that poll workers and others complied with all applicable chain-of-custody rules tracking ballots as they work their way through the system.[123]

Finally, once all the votes are cast, counted, canvassed, and—if the election was close—recounted and audited for accuracy, the results are certified and sent to the state's chief election officer, usually the secretary of state.[124] This has traditionally been a routine matter, although in recent years individuals have at times threatened to not certify results based on vague allegations of fraud or other election misconduct.[125] This is rarely (if ever) their role. Instead, all states have contest procedures or other rules enacted by their state legislatures, setting out the proper procedures for resolving disputes, usually through state courts.[126] In addition, there are state and federal laws penalizing election officials who refuse to fulfill these duties and authorizing alternative certification procedures that can be used if necessary.[127]

These extensive procedures ensure that our election systems are secure, but they are not infallible. In elections like those for the U.S. presidency, when more than 150 million votes are cast,[128] errors can and do occur. Fortunately, the multiple checks built into the system help ensure that these errors are caught and corrected. There are of course some bona fide instances of fraud or intentional manipulation of election results in the United States, but there is no evidence of widespread fraud in our elections today.[129]

There are, however, ample opportunities to sow distrust. Residents of a state requiring voters to request absentee ballots in advance and only for particular reason may find it appalling that a neighboring state automatically mails ballots to all active registered voters. Inaccuracies in voter registration rolls are amplified as "proof" that fraudulent votes were cast rather than seen as the normal consequence of lags in updating data and ensuring that eligible voters are not wrongly removed.[130] Voters in small jurisdictions accustomed to having results fully reported right after the polls close are suspicious of results coming in hours or days later from larger jurisdictions using centralized counting centers.[131] All of this virtually guarantees that fodder will be available for those who want to feed conspiracy theories and stoke distrust in the system.

There are sensible ways to address these problems. Obvious solutions include increasing cooperative efforts between state and federal agencies to secure electronic voter data,[132] supporting nationwide databases to provide more accurate and up-to-date information against which to check voter registration rolls,[133] providing funding for county election officials to replace old voting machines with newer ones using better and more secure software,[134] making changes to state laws to permit mailed-in ballots to be processed and counted in a more timely manner, and protecting election workers from threats and harassment.[135] A few states have adopted these reforms,[136] but others have gone the opposite direction and done things more likely to aggravate problems, such as giving nonexperts access to voting equipment,[137] requiring the hand counting of ballots,[138] and withdrawing from the nationwide data system that helps states ensure the accuracy of their voter rolls.[139]

Changes like these have heightened calls on Congress to use its Elections Clause power to enact new nationwide standards governing federal elections.[140] In today's political environment, any new federal laws will almost certainly be immediately challenged as beyond the scope of congressional power under Article I of the Constitution. As we've seen, though, that power is comprehensive and likely supports a broad range of federal rules. But Congress also has another source of power to point to when regulating elections, and it is a potent one: the Reconstruction Amendments adopted in the wake of the Civil War. These amendments dramatically changed the division of power between the federal and state governments, and few things were as affected by that shift as the operation of our elections. It is those developments we will turn to in the next chapter.

Five

Reconstructing the Republic

All of this is on account we want to register, to become first-class citizens, and if the Freedom Democratic Party is not seated now, I question America, is this America, the land of the free and the home of the brave where we have to sleep with our telephones off of the hooks because our lives be threatened daily because we want to live as decent human beings, in America?"

—FANNIE LOU HAMER, co-founder of the Mississippi Freedom Democratic Party, testifying in 1964 at the Democratic National Convention about the violent consequences faced by Black Americans attempting to register and vote[1]

When we think of America's founders most of us probably think of George Washington, Alexander Hamilton, James Madison, and the other men who met in Philadelphia in 1787 and drafted the original Constitution. But their constitution, in important ways, is not ours.[2] Their constitution disproportionately empowered slave states, failed to enfranchise most Americans, and allowed states to violate the rights of their own citizens. Our Constitution, in contrast, took root during what historian Eric Foner calls "the Second Founding"—the decade following the Civil War when men like John Bingham, Thaddeus Stevens, and Charles Sumner debated the Thirteenth, Fourteenth, and Fifteenth Amendments and reset the rules of American democracy.

Today, we refer to these amendments collectively as the Reconstruction Amendments. But they were not introduced or ratified as a group. Quite the contrary. Each of these critical amendments was adopted in distinct moments in time, and each was designed to accomplish different things. The Thirteenth prohibited slavery across the nation. The Fourteenth made citizens out of enslaved people, protected the rights of residents against their own states, and committed the federal government to safeguarding the equality of all Americans. The Fifteenth prohibited discrimination in voting on the basis of race. These changes promised to transform our system of government. And for a brief period of time, it *was* transformed. Across the former Confederacy, Black men streamed to the polls. They ran in and won elections. In South Carolina, a majority of members elected to the state legislature after the war were newly enfranchised Black men.[3] In other states, genuinely multiracial legislatures were elected for the first time.[4] Under the protection of the Union Army and with the authority of the United States government on its side, democracy in America seemed poised to thrive.

Instead, a violent backlash took root. Democratically elected governments were overthrown, elected officials were barred from taking office, and they and their supporters were threatened, beaten, and murdered.[5] The commitment of white northerners to Reconstruction, perhaps never terribly robust, waned.[6] Political compromises created legal ambiguities, generating more than a century of debate about the meaning of the Reconstruction Amendments. As we will see, it was clear that these amendments changed who "the people" were and how they would be represented in Congress and state legislatures around the country. But the extent to which they changed the balance of power between Congress and the states over the rules governing American elections was hotly contested.

This chapter examines these issues, specifically in relation to how the Reconstruction Congress that enacted these amendments expected them to restructure the institutions of American democracy and give Congress, rather than the states, power over how the new rights enshrined in the amendments would be protected. We'll examine the democracy-defining aspects of each of the amendments, early decisions of the Supreme Court limiting their reach, and later efforts by Congress to reassert its authority to enact laws under them. We will then turn to an in-depth look at the Voting Rights Act of 1965 (VRA) to better understand current debates about race and representation in America today.

————————

As we will see throughout this chapter, the Thirteenth, Fourteenth, and Fifteenth Amendments do different things in different ways. But they each do one important thing in the same way: They increase the power of Congress to make laws. It is a core tenet of our system that the federal government is a government of limited powers. Generally speaking, it can only act when authorized to do so by the Constitution. States, in contrast, are governments of plenary (general) powers. They can do anything the Constitution doesn't prohibit. The Reconstruction Amendments didn't change that basic design, but they did give Congress new power by authorizing it to enact laws enforcing the rights protected by the new amendments. Each of the amendments does this by including an "enforcement" provision giving Congress power to "enforce" the new constitutional rights through "appropriate" federal legislation.

The Supreme Court at times refers to these enforcement powers as "prophylactic."[7] Congress can use them to create a type of buffer zone around your rights by making it illegal for a state to do things that put those rights at risk, even when what the state is doing does not itself violate the Constitution. Congress, in other words, can make illegal things that are not themselves unconstitutional. This means that the substantive rights embodied in the Reconstruction Amendments are protected in two distinct ways. When a state does something that violates the right itself, the state has violated the Constitution and you can file a lawsuit demanding that it stop. That would be true whether or not Congress enacted any new laws. But under the enforcement provisions, Congress can also enact federal laws prohibiting state actors from doing things that run the risk of violating your rights in the first place. It can act *prophylactically* by making it illegal under federal law to do things that that threaten your rights, even before they are infringed.

What that means for our purposes is that the Reconstruction Amendments give Congress significantly more power than did the original Constitution to make laws regulating both federal and state elections. As we saw in the last chapter, the original Constitution gave Congress meaningful power in this area, including the power to override state laws regulating the times, places, and manner of federal elections. But it did not give the federal government any power over how states managed *state* elections, and even for federal elections it left with the states power to define the qualifications of their voters, draw legislative districts, and make (at least as an initial matter) many other rules involving both state and federal elections. The enforcement provisions of the Reconstruction Amendments readjust this allocation of responsibility by empowering Congress to enact additional federal laws, binding on the states in both state and federal elections, to prevent and punish violations of voting rights, especially—but, as we'll see in Chapter 6, not only—those that are racially discriminatory.

Many of the battles between Congress and the Supreme Court over the Reconstruction Amendments are about the scope of these new powers. Can Congress pass any law Congress considers appropriate to enforcing the underlying rights, or does the Court have to agree? If the Court does get a say, should it defer to congressional judgment in most cases or make its own independent assessment of the need for the federal law? Understanding how Congress and the Court have answered these questions over the century and a half since the Civil War is the first step toward exploring how these amendments changed who we are as a people and how we govern ourselves. So we will begin by learning a bit about each of these amendments, Congress's early efforts to enforce them, and the Supreme Court's initial response.

Of the three Reconstruction Amendments, the Thirteenth seems the most straightforward. Its first section reads simply: "Neither slavery nor involuntary servitude, except as a punishment for crime whereof the party shall have been duly convicted, shall exist within the United States, or any place subject to their jurisdiction." Section 2 then gives Congress the power to enforce the provisions of Section 1. Passed by Congress as the war was winding down and ratified in 1865 before the Confederate states were readmitted to the Union,[8] the Thirteenth Amendment ended chattel slavery throughout the nation.[9] But at least some of the men who advocated for its adoption believed that it did more.[10] Slavery was of course a brutal reality in antebellum America, but it also was used as a metaphor for domination.[11] In this sense, then, to be freed from slavery not only meant a literal release from bondage but also necessarily bestowed other rights and liberties enjoyed by free men.[12]

Just what those were, though, was unclear. The discourse of the day divided rights into different categories. Natural rights included rights such as life, liberty, and the right to enjoy the "fruits of one's own labor."[13] Civil rights included things like owning property, signing contracts, suing and being sued, and freedom of movement. Political rights included the right to vote and participate directly in self-government, while social rights involved the way people organized their private lives, things like the right to be educated and raise children.[14] These categories were not clear-cut, then or now,[15] but most supporters of the Thirteenth Amendment likely believed the amendment protected at least the natural and some civil rights of the freedmen.[16] The Civil Rights Act of 1866, enacted by Congress shortly after ratification of the Thirteenth Amendment, exemplifies this understanding.[17] In it, Congress made clear that all people born in the United States were citizens of the United States and, as such, had the right to make and enforce contracts, give evidence in court, hold and sell property, and enjoy "the full and equal benefit" of the law.[18]

In addition to ending slavery, then, the Thirteenth Amendment also provided at least some federally protected constitutional rights to the freedmen. But what it did not do was address the pressing question of whether and how those men would be represented in America's institutions of government.[19] Dealing with that question was left for after the war, when Congress begin grappling with the complex question of how to re-integrate the Confederate states into the reconstructed Union.

The compromises over slavery embedded in the 1787 Constitution made this a challenging task. As you will recall from Chapter 2, the Three-Fifths Compromise allowed slaveholding states to count enslaved people within those states as three-fifths of a person for purposes of allocating each state's representation in the House of Representatives. Since that allocation also effected the distribution among the states of electoral college votes, the three-fifths clause had effectively given slaveholding states disproportionate power in two of the three branches of the federal government. Emancipation had nullified the three-fifths clause. Since they were no longer enslaved, Black Americans would, like everyone else, now be counted as whole persons for purposes of these calculations. But if states retained the power given to them under the 1787 Constitution to define the qualifications of their voters, the net effect would be that white voters in southern states denying Black residents the right to vote would reenter the Union with even more disproportionate power than they had prior to the war.[20]

The Reconstruction Congress was awash with proposed amendments attempting to deal with this problem. They included amendments that would encourage southern states to enfranchise Black Americans by requiring that allocation of seats in the House of Representatives be based on a state's number of voters rather than the number of residents, to eliminate the Electoral College and elect the president through a national popular vote, and even to deal with the question directly by simply constitutionalizing the right of all adult men to vote.[21] But each of these options was controversial, even among congressional Republicans.[22] They were seen as too intrusive on states' prerogatives, too racially progressive, or simply too politically costly.[23]

So the Fourteenth Amendment as ultimately adopted by Congress took a different approach. Approved by Congress in 1866 and ratified two years later (including by reconstructed southern legislatures who were required to do so as a condition of readmission to the Union[24]), the Fourteenth Amendment is the longest amendment ever added to the U.S. Constitution. Today, the most well-known section of the amendment is probably Section 1, which establishes birthright citizenship, bars states from making or enforcing laws abridging the "privileges or immunities" of citizens of the United States, prohibits states from depriving people of "life, liberty, or property" without due process, and guarantees equal protection under law. Despite a few false starts from the Supreme Court, these provisions form the textual foundation for many of the rights that define us as Americans today. They prohibit most race and gender discrimination, guarantee marriage equality and other fundamental rights, and are the source of the entire body of constitutional law requiring state governments to comply with the Bill of Rights (which originally applied only to the federal government).[25]

In the 1860s, though, most of these developments lay far in the future. It was Section 2 of the amendment, not Section 1, that tried to deal with the immediately pressing challenge created by the nullification of the three-fifths clause. It did so *not* by constitutionalizing the right of all adult men to vote (a step that would continue to be debated even as the Fifteenth Amendment took shape) but instead by stripping states who refused to extend the franchise to most adult men of a portion of their representation in Congress. Specifically, Section 2 says that whenever the right to vote is denied to any adult male inhabitant of a state, other than as punishment for a crime, the state's representation in Congress "will be reduced" in the same proportion as the percentage of such men who are denied the ballot.

Like the three-fifths clause itself, this provision was yet another constitutional compromise, this time between congressmen who wanted to enfranchise Black men directly and those who wanted to leave the question of whether, and when, to extend the vote to formerly enslaved people within the discretion of the individual states.[26] The Section 2 compromise would leave voter qualifications, including race-based qualifications, in the hands of the states but punish those states that refused to extend the vote to the freedmen by reducing the state's representation in Congress. Unfortunately, this compromise also turned out to be a capitulation. Despite decades of almost complete Black disenfranchisement in the south, Congress never reduced the representation of any state, and Section 2 has become functionally dormant.[27]

Like Section 2, Section 3 is another a democracy-protecting provision of the Fourteenth Amendment that has had little effect, at least in modern times. Section 3 prohibits from holding most state or federal offices anyone who takes an oath of office to support the Constitution of the United States and then takes part in an insurrection or rebellion against the United States. It was designed to ensure that southern states would respect the newly won rights of freedmen by preventing Confederate oath-breakers from returning to positions of power.[28] The hope was that southern states, purged of their treasonous officials, could nurture a new generation of state leaders committed to the egalitarian goals of the Reconstruction Congress.[29]

Section 3 was mainly of historic interest until it was revived recently in response to the events of January 6, 2021. Citing Donald Trump's actions that day, Colorado invoked Section 3 to deny Trump access to the ballot in that year's presidential election.[30] Trump's role in organizing and inciting the crowd that breached the capital, they argued, rendered him constitutionally ineligible to serve as president under Section 3. The U.S. Supreme Court disagreed. In a per curium ("by the court") opinion, the justices unanimously held that only Congress could trigger Section 3 in federal elections. Since Congress had taken no action to disqualify Trump, states were powerless to do so themselves.[31] (Section 4, while not related to elections, also remains largely of historic interest. It absolved the United States of responsibility for debts incurred by the Confederacy, prohibited states and the federal government from compensating slaveholders for any losses associated with emancipation, and prohibited questioning the validity of any public debt of the United States.[32])

While Sections 2 and 3 were important for at least trying to restructure the institutions of American government to be more democratic and more representative, neither of them took the critical step of explicitly guaranteeing a right to vote. Black men had in fact been voting in the occupied southern states since the end of the Civil War, but they were doing so not as a matter of constitutional right but of statutory grace. A series of laws known as the Reconstruction Acts put the rebelling states under military control, required them to write new state constitutions enfranchising Black men, and tasked federal authorities with overseeing elections to ensure that the right to vote was protected.[33] As a result, in 1867, an astonishing 85 percent of adult Black men in the former Confederate states were registered to vote.[34]

But these protections were only statutory, and statutes can be repealed. They also were only in effect in states that had rebelled; their protections did not extend to Black Americans living in the north, in border states, or in other areas not covered by the acts. Black leaders and their allies, consequently, had advocated for years that the right to vote should be constitutionalized. Constitutionalizing their right to vote, they argued, was the surest way to protect both their freedom and their ability to participate as full and equal members in American democracy.[35] After the unexpectedly close election of 1868, Republicans in Congress, realizing that Black voters would be essential to their continued electoral success, finally agreed.[36] So the Reconstruction Congress went back to the drawing board one more time to put the freedmen's right to vote on more solid ground by amending the Constitution again, this time to directly protect voting rights.[37]

Congressional Republicans disagreed about exactly how what would become the Fifteenth Amendment should go about protecting those rights.[38] A key dispute was over whether the amendment should grant a positive right to vote or be just a negative prohibition against race-based discrimination in voting.[39] The difference was important. Advocates of an expansive approach understood that a provision narrowly focused on race discrimination could allow state legislatures to impose restrictions that were neutral on their face but nonetheless discriminated against Black voters (such as literacy tests or "grandfather clauses").[40] Advocates of a narrow approach, in contrast, worried that a broad amendment would encroach too much on state authority.[41] They also had a much more practical concern: They feared that an amendment constitutional-izing the right to vote couldn't be ratified.[42] An affirmative right to vote, they noted, would cast doubt on voter qualifications used in many northern states to deny the franchise to recent immigrants (most notably Irish Catholics), putting ratification in those states in doubt.[43] California and Oregon also were unlikely to support an amendment guaranteeing the vote to their growing Chinese populations.[44]

Given these concerns, the more cautious approach won. The Fifteenth Amendment does not expressly constitutionalize an affirmative right to vote. Instead, it says "the right of citizens of the United States to vote shall not be denied or abridged by the United States or by any State on account of race, color, or previous condition of servitude." That wording meant that states could continue to determine the qualifications of their voters, as long as those qualifications did not discriminate on any of the prohibited grounds. Like its two predecessors, the Fifteenth Amendment also included an enforcement provision, giving Congress power to enforce its provisions by appropriate legislation. The Nineteenth and Twenty-sixth Amendments, which decades later would prohibit discrimination in voting on the basis of sex (the Nineteenth) and age (the Twenty-sixth), would follow this same formula.

Even this narrower approach to voting rights proved controversial. The Fifteenth Amendment was quickly ratified by the Reconstruction legislatures sitting in the readmitted southern states and in most of the New England and midwestern states.[45] Georgia, which had been read-mitted to the Union in 1868 but then expelled again when its white rep-resentatives ejected newly elected Black representatives from the state legislature, ratified it as a condition of being re-readmitted.[46] But California, Oregon, and the border states refused to ratify.[47] New York did, but then tried to rescind its ratification, while the Indiana legislature ratified without meeting its own quorum requirements.[48] Despite these difficulties, the U.S. secretary of state announced on March 30, 1870, that the Fifteenth Amendment had been ratified.[49] The right of the freedmen to vote appeared, finally, to be on firmer constitutional ground.

It would be a short-lived victory. Within a few years, white southerners would embark on an unprecedented campaign of violence and intimidation, overthrowing the racially diverse legislatures elected after the end of the war and "redeeming" southern statehouses.[50] The Ku Klux Klan and other paramilitary groups would terrorize Black voters across the south. Union troops (and northern voters) would abandon the region, apparently as part of an agreement to settle the blood-soaked election of 1876.[51] By 1880, the state governments that had overseen the nation's first racially diverse democracies were gone.[52] By the early 1900s, Jim Crow laws enacted by all-white legislatures imposed rigid racial segregation on virtually every aspect of southern life.[53] Black voters were routinely denied the right to vote, and no southern state would send another Black representative to Congress until 1973.[54] America's first experiment in multiracial democracy lasted less than thirty years.

And the U.S. Supreme Court's cramped interpretation of the Reconstruction Amendments bears at least some of the blame.

———————

The Supreme Court's first opportunity to define the scope of the Reconstruction Amendments came in 1873, in *The Slaughter-House Cases*.[55] The underlying facts of the case had nothing to do with the rights of Black Americans, but the Court's decision in it would dramatically limit Congress's ability to use its new powers to protect those rights. *Slaughter-House* involved a challenge to a law regulating slaughterhouses in New Orleans. Slaughterhouse owners argued that the law violated the part of Section 1 of the Fourteenth Amendment that prohibits states from abridging the "privileges or immunities" of citizens of the United States.[56] The regulation, they argued, abridged their ability to practice their trade.[57] So the question presented to the Court was what privileges and immunities are protected by that clause.

Today, a court likely would reject a claim like this on the grounds that reasonable health and safety regulations are rarely unconstitutional under any provision of the Fourteenth Amendment.[58] The Supreme Court in *Slaughter-House* also rejected the claim, but for a very different reason. Interpreting the Privileges or Immunities Clause for the first time, the Court chose to read it as creating not one but two distinct categories of citizenship: state citizenship and federal citizenship.[59] It then went on to hold that the Fourteenth Amendment only protected the rights of federal citizenship.[60] So what rights were those? The authors of the Fourteenth Amendment may have thought they were a set of rights described in an earlier Supreme Court decision as "fundamental"—the rights essential to citizens of a free nation.[61] But the *Slaughter-House* justices took a different approach.

The rights of federal citizenship, the Court held, were *not* those deemed fundamental to the citizens of a free nation. Instead, federal citizenship rights included only those "owing their existence" to the federal government, such as the right to petition Congress and use U.S. seaports. The rich bundle of rights essential to freedom, the Court held, were a product of *state* rather than federal citizenship. So protecting those rights remained the exclusive responsibility of state governments, which meant Congress could not use its new enforcement powers to protect them.[62] The slaughterhouse owners lost their case, but Congress lost the power to enact legislation protecting a vast array of important civil and political rights through the Privileges or Immunities Clause.[63]

Ten years later, in *The Civil Rights Cases*, the Supreme Court again restricted the scope of congressional power to enforce the Reconstruction Amendments.[64] The law at issue this time was the Civil Rights Act of 1875, enacted by Congress under its power to enforce both the Thirteenth and Fourteenth Amendments.[65] The Civil Rights Act of 1875 is an extraordinary piece of legislation. Enacted more than 150 years ago, it prohibited discrimination on the basis of race in privately owned hotels, restaurants, and other places of "public amusement" (a legal term of art meaning, generally speaking, businesses open to the public[66]). Had it remained in effect and been enforced, it would have cast significant legal doubt on the entire sordid regime of Jim Crow. Instead, the Court struck it down as beyond Congress's power to enact under either the Thirteenth or the Fourteenth Amendment.

The Thirteenth Amendment argument is the most straightforward. The Thirteenth Amendment was (and is) understood to give Congress power to eradicate not just slavery itself but also the "badges and incidents" of slavery.[67] Unlike both the Fourteenth and the Fifteenth, the Thirteenth Amendment does not have what is called a "state action" requirement—the amendment's prohibitions restrain everyone, not just public or governmental officials.[68] The Reconstruction Congress therefore believed that the enforcement provision of the Thirteenth Amendment gave it power to prohibit race discrimination in privately owned places of public accommodation (like inns, hotels, and shops) as a way to eradicate the "incidents" of slavery, including private race discrimination.[69]

In *The Civil Rights Cases*, the Supreme Court rejected this argument. It did so by embracing a breathtakingly shallow understanding of the link between slavery and racism. It would be "running the slavery argument into the ground," the justices wrote a whopping eighteen years after the end of the Civil War, to consider private race discrimination an "incident" of more than two centuries of race-based slavery.[70] Consequently, the Court held, Congress had no power to regulate such discrimination under the enforcement provision of the Thirteenth Amendment.[71]

The Court also rejected Congress's argument that it could enact the law under the enforcement provision of the Fourteenth Amendment. The Fourteenth Amendment includes more substantive protections than does the Thirteenth. In addition to the Privileges or Immunities Clause, the Fourteenth Amendment includes the Equal Protection Clause, which bars states from denying people the "equal protection" of the law. In *The Civil Rights Cases*, Congress argued that it had authority to enact the

Civil Rights Act as a way to enforce that provision, regardless of whether it also could do so under the Thirteenth Amendment. States that failed to protect their Black citizens from private race discrimination, Congress argued, were denying those citizens the equal protection of the law, enabling Congress to use its enforcement powers to step in.[72]

Once again, the Court disagreed. Because the Fourteenth Amendment has a state action requirement, the substantive protection of the amendment only prohibits discrimination by state (governmental) actors. This meant that the hotel owners and shopkeepers regulated by the Civil Rights Act were not themselves violating the Fourteenth Amendment when they discriminated on the basis of race.[73] So the question presented to the Court was whether a state's *failure to prevent* private discrimination was nonetheless the type of state (in)action that could trigger Congress's enforcement power.

The Court held that it was not. Since private acts of race discrimination are not themselves unconstitutional, the Court said, Congress could not regulate those acts under the enforcement powers because there was no underlying unconstitutional act for Congress to remedy or prevent.[74] In other words, a state's failure to prevent private race discrimination was not a failure to provide equal protection because private discrimination itself did not itself violate the Fourteenth Amendment. In 1896 the Court would go even further, validating the "separate but equal" doctrine and holding in *Plessy v. Ferguson* that even state-mandated racial discrimination did not violate Equal Protection.[75] *Plessy*, and the legalized apartheid regime it ushered in, remained the law of the land for more than fifty years until it was finally overturned by *Brown v. Board of Education*.[76]

The Court's approach to voting rights under the Reconstruction Amendments fared no better. The scope of the Fifteenth Amendment was tested in 1875 in *United States v. Cruikshank*.[77] The facts underlying *Cruikshank* are bleak. In the aftermath of the 1872 election, a group of Black men in Colfax, Louisiana, gathered at the request of the local sheriff to protect elected officials from being forcibly removed from the county courthouse.[78] A mob of Klansmen and former Confederate soldiers arrived, surrounded the building, and set it on fire.[79] More than one hundred Black men were killed in the resulting violence, many apparently while fleeing the burning building or after surrendering to the mob.[80] Their murderers were caught and convicted in federal court under the Ku Klux Klan Act, a law enacted under the enforcement provision making it a federal crime to conspire to injure or threaten people with the intent of depriving them of their right to vote.[81]

The Supreme Court invalidated the convictions. The *Cruikshank* Court acknowledged that the right to vote *free from race discrimination* was a federal right guaranteed by the Fifteenth Amendment (a proposition difficult to deny, given the text of the amendment). Echoing *The Slaughter-House Cases*, though, the Court went on to say that the right to vote was *itself* a privilege of state, not federal, citizenship and could only be protected by state law.[82] Applying that distinction to the facts of the case before it, the Court noted that that the criminal indictment brought against the defendants had not specifically alleged that the victims had been attacked *because of* their race.[83] The indictment noted that the victims were "of African descent" and that the purpose of the attack was to deny them their right to vote, but it had not, according to the Court, sufficiently connected the dots between those two things. Their prosecution, the Court therefore concluded, was enforcing the right to vote, not the right to vote free of race discrimination. Since the generic right to vote was a right of state rather than federal citizenship, the perpetrators of the Colfax Massacre could not be prosecuted under the Ku Klux Klan Act.[84]

For all of its problems, *Cruikshank* did seem to leave the door open to federal prosecution under more carefully drafted indictments. But even that door was closed a few years later, in *Giles v. Harris* (1903).[85] Jackson Giles was an eligible voter living in Montgomery, Alabama. A Black man, he had voted in Montgomery since the end of the Civil War—more than thirty years.[86] But after the end of Reconstruction and the dismantling of the reconstructed state legislature in Alabama, a subsequent state legislature had enacted a new state constitution imposing a dizzying array of voter registration rules. When Giles attempted to register under those rules, his registration was rejected.[87] He sued, arguing that Alabama's registration rules violated the Fifteenth Amendment by denying him the right to vote on the basis of race.

It may not be a surprise at this point to learn that the Supreme Court rejected this claim as well. The Court, in a decision written by Oliver Wendell Holmes, did not shrink from the reality of what was happening to Giles and thousands of other Black Americans across the former Confederate states. The purpose and effect of Alabama's new registration rules, the Court acknowledged, was to deny the Black citizens of Alabama the right to vote.[88] So the rules should have been right in the bull's-eye of things the Fifteenth Amendment both prohibits and empowers the federal government to prevent. But to the justices, that was precisely the problem. Giles's accusation, Justice Holmes wrote for the Court, implicated the entire voter registration scheme set out in the Alabama constitution.[89] Since the Court could not possibly provide relief to *all* of Alabama's unconstitutionally rejected registrants, he reasoned, ordering Giles to be registered would involve the Court in a "fraud on the United States."[90] The Court refused to sully its hands in such a way, opting instead to leave Giles without a remedy or a vote.

If the election of 1876 ended political reconstruction, *Slaughter-House*, *The Civil Rights Cases*, *Cruikshank*, and *Giles* ended its legal counterpart. *Slaughter-House* shut down the Privileges or Immunities Clause as a meaningful source of constitutionally protected rights. *The Civil Rights Cases* left Congress helpless to act against private race discrimination, even when state governments refused to do so themselves. *Cruikshank* and *Giles* essentially removed federal court review of most claims of systemic race discrimination in state voting systems. In each of these cases, the Court embraced a stingy view of the substantive rights protected by the Reconstruction Amendments and of the powers given to Congress to enforce them. Together, they eviscerated the Reconstruction Amendments and hampered the ability of the federal government to protect the hard-won rights of Black Americans.

Cruikshank and *Giles* are widely reviled today, but the state action doctrine as defined in *The Civil Rights Cases'* and *Slaughter-House's* cramped understanding of the Privileges or Immunities Clause remain the law of the land.[91] Why would the Supreme Court take such a limited view of these amendments in the decades immediately following the war? The simplest explanation may be the most likely. The Republican Party's commitment to Reconstruction had flagged and the justices, like white Americans in both the north and the south, were ready to put the war behind them, even at the cost of the rights of Black Americans.[92] In addition, of course, the men who wrote and ratified the Reconstruction Amendments, like the authors of the original Constitution, had different ideas about what the new amendments would accomplish, and how. That left room for disagreement about what the words they wrote meant in the context of concrete cases. Nonetheless, it does seem unlikely that the nation's second founders would have believed they had fought so hard for so little. After the nation's bloodiest war, the assassination of a president, more than a decade of Reconstruction, and three constitutional amendments, Black Americans had gained their freedom but little else.

———

It would be more than half a century before Congress would again breathe life into the Reconstruction Amendments. In 1964, Congress used its power to regulate interstate commerce to pass the Civil Rights Act of 1964,[93] reenacting many of the same protections against private discrimination invalidated by the Supreme Court in *The Civil Rights Cases*.[94] More pertinently for our purposes, a year later Congress used its enforcement powers to pass the Voting Rights Act of 1965.[95]

The Voting Rights Act (VRA) was the culmination of decades of activism by citizens and civil rights groups working to secure voting rights. It prohibits any state (or their subdivisions, like towns and counties) from using any "voting qualification, or prerequisite to voting, or standard, practice, or procedure" to deny or abridge the right of any citizen of the

United States to vote on account of race.[96] As enacted, it barred jurisdictions with a history of race discrimination in voting from changing their voting procedures without first demonstrating that the change would not have a racially discriminatory effect and was not adopted with a racially discriminatory purpose.[97] It bans the use of literacy tests and similar mechanisms that had prevented Black Americans from registering and voting for decades.[98] It also makes it a federal crime to threaten people for voting or attempting to vote, authorizes the U.S. attorney general to enforce the rights protected by the law, and gives federal courts the power to ensure that the law is followed.[99]

Like Congress's earlier efforts to protect voting rights, the VRA was immediately challenged as beyond the scope of congressional power to enact under the Reconstruction Amendments.[100] But this time the Supreme Court upheld the law. In *South Carolina v. Katzenbach* the Court rejected the restrictive understanding of congressional power that its predecessors had embraced in cases like *Cruikshank* and *Giles*. Instead, it deferred to congressional judgment about what laws are necessary to protect the right to vote free from racial discrimination.[101] Chief Justice Earl Warren, citing a famous decision from 1819, wrote that as long as the goal of the law was legitimate and within the letter and spirit of the Constitution, Congress could take actions it deemed appropriate to enforce the Fifteenth Amendment.[102]

Applying that standard to the VRA, the Court in *Katzenbach* ruled that the extraordinary resistance that southern states had for decades shown to Black voting rights made even the most sweeping provisions of the VRA an appropriate—and therefore constitutional—response.[103] The Court reiterated this deferential approach to congressional power just a few months later, in another case involving the VRA, *Katzenbach v. Morgan*, noting that rigorous second-guessing of congressional judgments in this realm would "depreciate both congressional resourcefulness and congressional responsibility for implementing" voting rights.[104]

The impact of the VRA was immediate and dramatic. Banning the tests and devices used to disenfranchise Black Americans since the turn of the century, combined with federal oversight of registration proce-dures, resulted in a surge of Black voter registrations.[105] According to one estimate, more than 1.5 million Black Americans registered to vote in the south between 1966 and 1972.[106] By 1967, more than 50 percent of the Black voting-age population in the former Confederate states was registered, rates not seen since Reconstruction.[107] In Mississippi, Black voter registration skyrocketed from less than 10 percent to 60 percent.[108] In Virginia, the registration gap between Black and white voters virtually disappeared.[109] Black candidates once again began run-ning for and winning state and local elections, including in towns and cities where Black majorities were for the first time in more than eight decades able to exercise real electoral power and elect representatives of their choice.[110]

Once again, though, there was a backlash. This time, instead of di-rectly denying Black Americans the right to vote, jurisdictions devised methods to diminish their voting powers even when they were legally allowed to cast their ballots. One of the most effective ways of doing this was by manipulating legislative district boundaries.[111] We saw in Chap-ter 2 how population-malapportioned districts can skew representational equality by diluting the voting power of voters in high-population dis-tricts. After passage of the VRA, some jurisdictions turned to similar tac-tics to dilute the voting power of Black Americans, even while complying with the equal-population rule mandated by *Reynolds v. Sims*.

Some examples will help us see how this works.

Imagine a city whose voters are 45 percent Black and 55 percent white. Assume that the voting preferences of Black and white voters in this city are "racially polarized," meaning Black and white voters have a strong tendency to prefer different candidates. Then assume that hous-ing patterns in the city are racially segregated: Whether for historic or ongoing reasons, Black and white residents tend to live in different neigh-borhoods. Finally, imagine a city council composed of nine elected rep-resentatives. If the voting power in this hypothetical city is distributed roughly equally, candidates preferred by Black voters would probably win four of the nine seats (45 percent) while candidates preferred by white voters would likely win the other five (55 percent).[112]

Now imagine different ways these voters could be grouped together for purposes of electing the city council members. The city could decide to elect every member of the council "at large." There are various ways of structuring at-large elections, but our city decides to do it by letting every voter vote for all nine council members. If voting is racially polarized, the candidates preferred by the white voters will win every single seat with 55 percent of the vote each.

Alternatively, our city could elect its council members through districts but draw the district lines to generate an equally inequitable result. Imagine that in our city the racially segregated neighborhoods tend to run from east to west (like a tic-tac-toe board with all X's in the top and bottom rows, and all O's in the middle row). By drawing districts vertically (north to south) rather than horizontally (east to west), the city could "crack" Black voters so even though they make up 45 percent of the population overall, they don't constitute a majority of voters in any district. In this scenario, white voters would again be able to elect 100 percent of the members of the city council because they would constitute a voting majority in each district.

Finally, our city also could dilute Black voting power by doing exactly the opposite. It could "pack" Black voters into just a few districts, concentrating them into the minimum number of districts possible under *Reynolds*. In this scenario, a candidate preferred by Black voters would win those districts resoundingly, but Black voters would have little influence in the other districts. In election-law lingo, the votes of a large number of Black voters (every vote over the number necessary to win the seat) would be "wasted." This scheme would ensure that Black voters could elect one or two members of the nine members of the council but would still leave them underrepresented on the council overall relative to their proportion of the population.

Obviously, these examples are overly simplified. Residential housing is not crisply racially segregated, and of course not all voters of the same race share the same political preferences. But when racially polarized voting and segregated housing patterns do exist, electoral design choices like at-large voting, cracking voters, and packing voters can dilute the voting power of racial minorities as effectively as denying them access to the ballot in the first place. That is the problem the Supreme Court grappled with in 1985, in a case called *Thornburg v. Gingles.*[113]

Gingles grew out of a legislative districting plan enacted in North Carolina.[114] The plan relied on a mix of single-member and multi-member districts (a multi-member district is one in which a larger number of voters elect more than one representative). The challengers argued that the districts were drawn in areas where there were enough Black voters to constitute a majority in a single-member district and that the state had violated the VRA by instead drawing the districts so Black voters did not constitute a majority in any of them.[115] The claim, in other words, was that the districts were drawn like the tic-tac-toe example: They unnecessarily submerged Black voters into districts in which white voters were a majority, even though housing patterns would have enabled the legislature to draw several single-member districts in which Black voters would have been a majority.[116]

So the question for the Court in *Gingles* was whether this way of grouping people together for the purpose of electing representatives violated the VRA. If the districting scheme intentionally discriminated on the basis of race it could have been struck down as a direct violation of the Fifteenth Amendment. But Congress had used its power under the enforcement provision of the Fifteenth Amendment to regulate in the buffer zone by making it illegal under the VRA for states to apply voting rules with discriminatory *effects*, regardless of whether they were also adopted for a discriminatory *purpose* (which can be difficult to prove as a constitutional matter). Section 2 of the VRA does this by specifying that a law has a discriminatory effect, and therefore violates the statute, when minority voters have less opportunity than others to elect representatives of their choice.[117] The task facing the *Gingles* Court was how to apply this language to districting schemes like that enacted by North Carolina.

The test the Court set out in *Gingles* has been critical to ensuring that members of racial minority groups are able to elect representatives of their choice, as long as certain racially salient conditions continue to be part of American life. Under the Court's test, a legislative districting plan is likely to violate Section 2 if the challengers can show three things: that they are a large and sufficiently geographically concentrated group to constitute a majority of voters in a single-member district; that members of the group are politically cohesive; and that voters who are not members of the minority group engage in bloc voting sufficient to defeat the minority group's candidate of choice in most cases.[118] As a practical matter, what this test means is that in areas where segregated housing patterns and racially polarized voting persist, a sufficiently large minority population will usually have a statutory entitlement to a "majority-minority" district—a district in which a majority of voters are members of the racial minority group. *Gingles*, in short, helps ensure that nonwhite voters can win representation as long as race remains relevant in American life, at least as evidenced by racially divided housing and voting patterns.

The Supreme Court has applied this interpretation of Section 2 many times in the decades since *Gingles* was decided, and hundreds of representatives have been elected to Congress and state legislatures in "Section 2" districts.[119] It is one of the primary mechanisms ensuring that Americans of color are represented in the nation's legislative bodies today. But it has always been controversial. As we have seen throughout this book, how we group people together for purposes of dividing up political representation matters. Allocating representation in the U.S. Senate by state instead of population give votes in small-population states more power than those in larger states. Counting children when dividing up seats in the House of Representatives gives voters in districts with large numbers of kids more voting weight than voters in other districts. Electing the president through the Electoral College rather than a direct popular vote gives voters in swing states more influence over who becomes president than is enjoyed by voters in other states.

Yet in a representative democracy, choices like these are unavoidable.

Which means the most relevant legal question in such situations often is not just what decision is made, but who has the authority to make it. In terms of race and redistricting, the enforcement provisions of the Reconstruction Amendments give that power to Congress, and the Voting Rights Act represents Congress's judgment that certain racial considerations continue to deserve our attention when allocating representation in America today. But the Supreme Court has grown increasingly skeptical of laws taking race into account in any way, even when done to safeguard the rights of Black Americans.[120] This skepticism was evident in 2013, in a case called *Shelby County v. Holder*,[121] when the Court struck down a different section of the VRA as beyond the scope of Congress's enforcement powers. *Shelby County* is a complicated case, but it provides helpful insight into the current Court's understanding of congressional power to enforce the Reconstruction Amendments today.

Shelby County involved the so-called preclearance process created by Sections 4 and 5 of the VRA. These provisions required certain state and local governments (including Shelby County, Alabama) to get advance permission (preclearance) before they changed their election rules. They were included in the VRA to solve a specific problem. In addition to using tests and devices to prevent Black Americans from voting, state and local actors also had been weaponizing the time and expense of litigation to strip even hard-won legal victories of their value.[122] As soon as one racially discriminatory voting rule or practice was struck down as unconstitutional, unrepentant officials would simply tweak the law and force challengers to start the litigation process all over again.[123]

The preclearance process was designed to end that. Section 4 set out a "coverage formula" determining which states and jurisdictions would have to go through the pre-clearance process. As first enacted, the jurisdictions covered by the formula were those that had used tests or devices (like literacy tests) as a prerequisite to voting and had a turnout or registration rate of less than 50 percent of eligible voters in the 1964 presidential election (later updated to 1972).[124] The formula originally covered all of Georgia, Alabama, Louisiana, Mississippi, South Carolina, and

Virginia, as well as parts of North Carolina and Arizona.[125] Amendments to the formula to protect language minorities later brought parts of California, New York, Texas, Alaska, Florida, Michigan, and South Dakota into the process as well.[126]

Section 5 of the VRA then prohibited covered jurisdictions from changing their voting procedures unless they could first demonstrate that the change didn't have a racially discriminatory purpose and wouldn't have a racially discriminating effect.[127] This is different from how legal challenges usually work. Usually, states adopt whatever rules they want, and people who think a particular law is unconstitutional or otherwise invalid can then challenge it in court. The pre-clearance process flips that sequence on its head. Rather than require a litigant to file a lawsuit challenging a new rule after it is adopted, under the VRA government officials in covered jurisdictions had to prove in advance that their proposed rule change wasn't discriminatory. By reversing the burden of litigation this way, Section 5 aimed to stop the legal maneuvering that had disenfranchised voters so effectively before the VRA was enacted.[128]

The coverage formula and preclearance process had been upheld by the Supreme Court in 1966 as an appropriate use of Congress's enforcement powers.[129] But by the time *Shelby County* was decided in 2013, a majority of the justices decided things had changed.[130] Rather than grant Congress the same broad deference Chief Justice Warren had when first upholding the VRA, the Court in *Shelby County* imposed new constraints on congressional power. Instead of permitting Congress to enact any appropriate laws within the "letter and spirit" of the Constitution, Chief Justice John Roberts's majority opinion required Congress to demonstrate that extraordinary provisions like the preclearance process were responsive to "current" conditions.[131] The coverage formula, according to the Court, failed this test. Because it was based on decades-old data, it was not, in the Court's view, sufficiently calibrated to justify the different treatment it imposed on the covered jurisdictions.[132] Like *Cruikshank*, *Shelby County* left open the possibility that more careful drafting could resolve the constitutional problem. But it nonetheless is a clear signal that today's Court will not be shy about asserting its views of race and representation when judging congressional power to enforce the Reconstruction Amendments.

This apparent judicial willingness to second-guess Congress already has unleashed a flurry of challenges to Section 2 of the VRA.[133] Section 2 was not directly affected by the Court's holding in *Shelby County*, but its provisions are vulnerable to the same type of arguments. Recall that under current law, the Constitution itself is not violated unless a challenger can show that the government action at issue was taken with a discriminatory purpose and has a discriminatory effect.[134] But Section 2 of the VRA focuses exclusively on discriminatory effects. Unlike the Constitution, it is violated regardless of whether the state actor *intended* to discriminate on the basis of race. Using similar reasoning to that embraced by the Court in *Shelby County* and *The Civil Rights Cases*, opponents of Section 2 argue that it exceeds congressional power to use an effects-only test to "enforce" a right that itself requires a showing of discriminatory purpose.[135] A deeply divided Court upheld the effects test in 2023, but a future Court might well find that this is beyond the buffer zone given to Congress to enact laws under the enforcement provisions of the Reconstruction Amendments.[136]

Section 2 also is vulnerable to challenge on the grounds that it is itself unconstitutional, at least as construed in *Gingles*.[137] The argument here is that even if laws like the VRA generally speaking are within Congress's power to enact, Congress cannot enact this particular law because its focus on race-based districting violates the Equal Protection Clause of the Fourteenth Amendment. Under the Equal Protection Clause, governmental actors can only use race in their official decision-making when they have a really good (compelling) reason to do so, and if they do so in the narrowest possible way.[138] This tough test is why most uses of race by government officials are unconstitutional. That has obvious implications for a law like the VRA. The VRA is inherently race-based. It is designed to ensure that members of racial minority groups have an equal opportunity to participate in the political process and elect representatives of their choice. It not only permits governmental actors to pay attention to race when doing things like drawing legislative districts, it requires them to do so. Which means its constitutionality depends to some extent on what the justices believe about the relationship between race and representation in America today.

So far, the Court has upheld the VRA as an appropriate way to enforce the rights protected by the Reconstruction Amendments.[139] But a Supreme Court willing to second-guess congressional judgment about the extent to which race-based discrimination remains a salient problem in America today may very well take a different approach in the not-so-distant future.

———

The Thirteenth, Fourteenth, and Fifteenth Amendments fundamentally changed democracy in America. They promised that "we the people" would include not just men like those who wrote our original founding documents, but also men of color and even—eventually—women. They guaranteed the right to vote without regard to race and gave the federal government the power to protect that right. They enabled Congress to ensure that more of us would be represented in legislative bodies across the nation and created a template for generations of excluded Americans to follow when claiming their right to participate as full and equal citizens in our democratic republic. The amendments did not resolve all of America's questions about who is entitled to participate in self-government, how representation is divided, and who gets to decide, but they changed the terms of the debate and pointed us all more firmly in the direction of a fairer, more equitable system of government.

As we will see in the next chapter, one of these amendments—the Fourteenth—also has had implications for one of the most contested issues in American election law today: the extent to which state legislatures can enact laws making it more difficult for all of us, regardless of race, to vote by imposing burdens on how we register and cast our ballots.

Six

Protecting the Right to Vote

The true and only true basis of representative government is equality of rights. Every man has a right to one vote, and no more in the choice of representatives. The rich have no more right to exclude the poor from the right of voting, or of electing and being elected, than the poor have to exclude the rich; . . . It is always to be taken for granted, that those who oppose an equality of rights never mean the exclusion should take place on themselves.

—THOMAS PAINE, Dissertation on the
First Principles of Government, 1795[1]

Imagine for a moment that you are a prospective voter in Louisiana in the 1950s. You show up at a voter registration office. But instead of showing your identification and registering, you're handed a pencil and an exam and told you have ten minutes to complete it. You're also told the exam will be graded by the person administering it, and if you get a single question wrong you won't be allowed to register. When you start the test, you find thirty questions like this:

1. Draw a line around the number or letter of this sentence.

2. Draw a figure that is square in shape. Divide it in half by drawing a straight line from its northeast corner to its southwest corner, and

then divide it once more by drawing a broken line from the middle of its western side to the middle of its eastern side.

3. Write right from the left to the right as you see it spelled here.

How do you answer these questions? Is it possible to draw a *line* around a number or letter? Do words like "northeast" mean the top right corner of the piece of paper you are writing on, or the actual geography of your location? And what word is the right word to write in the final question?

These examples aren't made up. They're taken from an actual test administered in Louisiana in the 1950s.[2] In the first half of the twentieth century, tests like these often were used in racially discriminatory ways. Their inherent subjectivity enabled election officials to "fail" Black voters for virtually any reason while permitting white voters to register. But what if the Louisiana test was *not* used in a racially discriminatory way? Does anything in the Constitution prevent a state from making voters jump through hoops like these before they can exercise their fundamental right to vote?

This may be one of the most important questions facing American courts today. Despite the lack of evidence that voter fraud is a significant problem in American elections, inflated fears of rampant fraud have led state legislatures across the country to enact increasingly draconian restrictions on the right to vote. Many of these laws are extremely punitive. Election administrators, voter registration groups, and voters themselves are threatened with prosecution for even unintentional errors made while navigating all the new rules and regulations.[3] These laws are usually enacted on a partisan basis and can have racially discriminatory effects.[4] But partisan motivations are not treated as illegitimate by the Supreme Court, and racial discrimination is only unconstitutional when intentional, which can be hard to prove as a matter of law. The Voting Rights Act offers some protection against laws with racially discriminatory effects, but those protections are weak outside of the legislative districting context, and, as discussed in the previous chapter, may not survive long even there.[5]

So does anything limit the ability of states to enact these types of laws? That is the question we explore in this chapter, by considering how the Equal Protection Clause of the Fourteenth Amendment does and does not restrict the power of states to burden the right to vote through generally applicable, nondiscriminatory (in the constitutional sense) laws.

———————

Unlike in most modern democracies, there is no textually explicit right to vote in the U.S. Constitution. As we saw in the previous chapter, the Fifteenth Amendment prohibits states from denying or abridging the right to vote on account of race. The Nineteenth and Twenty-sixth Amendments do the same on the basis of sex and age, at least for people over the age of eighteen. But none of these amendments bestow an *affirmative* right to vote. Instead, they are anti-discrimination provisions. States remain constitutionally empowered to determine the "qualifications" of their voters (see Chapter 4) but are constitutionally prohibited from distinguishing among those voters on any of the prohibited grounds.

But that doesn't mean states can throw whatever hurdles they want in front of voters trying to exercise their right to vote. The Equal Protection Clause does impose some modest limitations. Those limitations have been clarified over several decades, as the modern Court's equal protection jurisprudence gradually took shape. Understanding those limits therefore requires us first to take a close look at what "equal protection" of the laws means under current law.

The Equal Protection Clause says "No state shall . . . deny to any person within its jurisdiction the equal protection of the laws."[6] At first blush, this may seem like a straightforward provision requiring states to treat everyone the same. But that can't be literally true. Laws treat people differently all the time. People in different income brackets pay different tax rates, people who are eighteen years old can enter into legally binding contracts but five-year-olds cannot, and people who jaywalk get fined while people who don't, don't. At its most basic level, what law *does* is draw distinctions between people and treat them differently based on those distinctions.

So the Equal Protection Clause cannot and does not prohibit states from engaging in the basic lawmaking function of drawing legal classifications that treat people differently. Instead, the Court has understood the clause to require different types of justifications for different types of classifications. Laws drawing routine classifications (like punishing jaywalkers but not more obedient pedestrians) are subject to very little judicial review. But laws drawn on what the Court calls "suspect classifications" are subject to more rigorous scrutiny. The Court has not settled on a clear test to determine what classifications are suspect, but classifications considered suspect include those that treat people differently on the basis of race, gender, ethnicity, and religion—classifications that too often rest on stereotypes or biases and that the Court therefore has reason to doubt are really necessary to accomplish the state's goals. The point of applying a more demanding test to this type of law is to ensure that states have good reasons for enacting laws using classifications like these.

To better understand how this works, consider two laws. One prohibits people under the age of twelve from entering into legally binding contracts without a parent's permission. The other prohibits women from entering into legally binding contacts without their spouse's permission. Both of these laws create different categories of people and treat the people in those categories differently. Young kids and women can't enter into contracts, but older people and men can. Even without any legal training, you probably won't be surprised to hear courts view the constitutionality of these two laws very differently. The law prohibiting women from entering into contracts will be much more closely scrutinized, and is much more likely to be unconstitutional, then the law prohibiting children from doing so. That's because gender is a suspect classification, but youth is not.

Doctrinally, lawyers call this "tiered review." While there is a great deal of variability in how the doctrine is actually used, it can be generally summarized as follows. Under the lowest tier of review (which applies to most laws) the challenged law will be constitutional as long as the state can show that it is *rationally* related to a *legitimate* state interest. Laws subject to this type of review are almost always constitutional and are rarely even challenged because the challenger is almost certain to lose. Laws drawing suspect classifications, on the other hand, are subject to the highest form of review, called "strict scrutiny." (Technically, gender-based distinctions are subject to a slightly different standard called "intermediate" review, but we can and will ignore that for our purposes.)[7] Under strict scrutiny review, a law will pass constitutional muster only if the state can show that the challenged law is advancing a *compelling* interest and that the classification is *narrowly tailored* to advance that interest. This is a tough test, and most laws subject to it are unconstitutional. So under this system of tiered review, a law prohibiting children from entering binding contracts would be unlikely to violate the Equal Protection Clause, but a law denying adult women the power to do so almost certainly would.[8]

Importantly, though, laws drawing suspect classifications are not the only ones subject to strict scrutiny review under the Equal Protection Clause. Courts also apply strict scrutiny to laws that affect the *fundamental rights* of some individuals but not others. As noted earlier, the Court's fundamental rights doctrine also is complicated, but the Court has consistently recognized that voting is a fundamental right. Consequently, under what lawyers call the "black letter law" of the Equal Protection Clause (the basic rules that form the starting point of any legal analysis), laws that hamper the ability of some people but not others to exercise their right to vote would be subject to strict scrutiny review, even when the classification drawn in the law is not suspect.

In theory, that should mean virtually all rules unequally affecting people's right to vote are subject to strict scrutiny and presumptively unconstitutional. But it doesn't actually work that way, and for a pretty good reason. Elections are state functions. We *need* laws governing how we run our elections. As we saw in Chapter 4, states routinely enact laws governing things like what names to print on ballots, how poll books are maintained and updated, where to locate polling places, and how to staff them. Every one of these laws will affect different voters differently. If our state assigns me to a polling place a block from my house but assigns you to one five miles from yours, your right to vote has been affected differently than mine. If one county decides to have seven days of early voting but another opts for fourteen days, the right to vote of people in the first county is burdened in a way that the right to vote of people in the second county is not.

Applying strict scrutiny to all of these types of rules would be a massive injection of federal courts into the endless number of choices states make when deciding how to administer elections. Judges are ill-suited for such a task. Do we really want courts invalidating election rules as a matter of constitutional law on the grounds that the state could have accomplished its goals by putting a particular polling place someplace else, or keeping polls open until eight p.m. instead of seven p.m.? There certainly are situations where this type of detailed oversight is necessary and appropriate, but applying strict scrutiny review to *every* decision about election administration would wreak havoc on the system.

So even though voting is a fundamental right, and even though state laws affecting fundamental rights are in theory subject to strict scrutiny review, strict scrutiny is not in fact applied to most routine election laws. Instead, the Supreme Court has developed a different set of tests to determine when generally applicable, nondiscriminatory rules regulating voting violate the Equal Protection Clause.

The Supreme Court's approach to this type of law can be explained by looking at three cases.

The first, *Harper v. Virginia*, is a 1966 case about the types of barriers states can impose when regulating access to the ballot.[9] The second, *Bush v. Gore*, is the infamous case that decided the 2000 presidential election and was the Court's first foray into imposing constitutional limitations on nuts-and-bolts administrative decisions about how votes are cast and counted.[10] The third, *Crawford v. Marion County Election Board*, was decided in 2008 and sets out the doctrine governing many of today's controversies involving the balance between election security and voter access.[11] Collectively, these cases illustrate how the Court applies equal protection doctrine to nondiscriminatory but burdensome restrictions on voting.

———————

We will start with *Harper*. *Harper* involved a Virginia law imposing a "poll tax" on voters. If you wanted to vote in a state election in Virginia—like an election for governor—you had to pay this tax six months before the election. It also required voters who hadn't voted recently to pay up to three years of back taxes for the years the voter missed. The tax was $1.50 in 1966, which is about $15 today. But it was only assessed on voters: If you wanted to vote, you had to pay this special tax, and if you didn't pay you couldn't vote.[12]

It sounds counterintuitive to contemporary ears, but when they were first introduced in this country poll taxes were actually used to *expand* the franchise. Before the Revolutionary War, only (white, male) landowners could vote in most colonies.[13] Poll taxes enacted after independence expanded the franchise by enabling white men who didn't own property to vote by paying the tax instead.[14] But the revival of poll taxes after the Civil War was very different. As many of its critics had foreseen, framing the Fifteenth Amendment as a negative right against discrimination rather than a positive right to vote invited states to enact restrictive voting laws that were not racially discriminatory on their face but nonetheless disenfranchised most Black voters.[15] Southern states recognized this and began passing laws imposing things like literacy tests and poll taxes that disproportionately disenfranchise Black voters.[16] Today, facial neutrality would not save an intentionally discriminatory law from strict scrutiny review,[17] but as we have seen, courts in the late 1800s and early 1900s had little interest in vigorously enforcing the Reconstruction Amendments. The rapid spread of poll taxes was one of the results.[18]

But poll taxes also kept poor white people from voting. By 1966, this had made them sufficiently unpopular that all but five states (Alabama, Mississippi, Texas, Arkansas, and Virginia) had abolished them entirely.[19] The Twenty-fourth Amendment, adopted in 1964, also had barred their use in federal (but not state) elections, and the Voting Rights Act of 1965 empowered the U.S. attorney general to sue states that used them to discriminate against Black voters in either state or federal elections.[20] But none of these provisions addressed the use of *non*discriminatory poll taxes in state elections in states, like Virginia, that continued to use them. So the question presented in *Harper* was whether those states could impose a generally applicable poll tax in state elections when that tax was not maintained for a racially discriminatory purpose or applied in a racially discriminatory way.[21]

The challengers argued that the poll tax violated the Equal Protection Clause by distinguishing between voters (treating them differently) based on their ability to pay the tax. This type of claim was not completely novel. As early as 1886 the Supreme Court had recognized that the question of whether nondiscriminatory voting regulations were "reasonable" was subject to judicial review.[22] In 1937, the Court heard but rejected an equal protection case challenging the constitutionality of a Georgia law imposing a poll tax on most men but not on women, minors, or the elderly.[23] In 1959, the Court held that the Equal Protection Clause wasn't violated when North Carolina applied a literacy test in a non–racially discriminatory way, because literacy was related to what the majority opinion called the "intelligent use of the ballot."[24] And in 1965, in *Carrington v. Rash*, the Court struck down a Texas law denying the right to vote to military personnel, on the grounds that the law was not sufficiently tailored to apply only to members of the military who were not bona fide state residents.[25]

Although not fully developed, the basic structure of modern equal protection analysis is visible in these early cases. The Court, in essence, asks if the state's asserted interest in the law is sufficiently strong to justify treating different groups of people (women, illiterate individuals, and soldiers) differently than other groups of people (most men, literate individuals, and civilians). While the first two cases would almost certainly come out differently today (literacy tests were outlawed nationwide under the VRA, and giving special consideration to women in the form of a gender-based tax break would no longer been seen as compatible with equal treatment), the bones of the modern doctrine were already in place by the time *Harper* was decided.

But it was *Harper* that added meat to those bones. In the earlier cases, the Court had been fairly deferential to the state's asserted need for the law at issue. Even in *Carrington*, the only one of the three decided in favor of the voter, the Court took care to point out that a better-designed law would likely pass constitutional muster. That type of deference to state legislatures was nowhere to be seen in *Harper*. The language of *Harper* was equivocal about what level of review the Court was applying, but the willingness of the Court to closely scrutinize the law was clear. "Voter qualifications," Justice William Douglas announced for the majority, "have no relation to wealth nor to paying or not paying this or any other tax." In addition, he wrote, poll taxes "introduce a capricious or irrelevant factor" into the electoral system.[26] Consequently, he concluded, the Equal Protection Clause is violated whenever a state makes the wealth of a voter or payment of a fee a prerequisite to voting.[27]

As the dissenting justices were quick to point out, Justice Douglas could only reach this conclusion by discounting the state's asserted interests in imposing the poll tax. Virginia had argued that the tax was important both because it facilitated the state's need to generate revenue and because it advanced the state's belief that taxpayers are more invested than nontaxpayers in the state's welfare.[28] The dissenters argued that the Court should defer to those interests as long as they were rational and not arbitrary. Justice Harlan, who wrote one of the dissents, believed that Virginia's justifications easily passed that test. After all, he argued, it had long been considered rational for a state to assume that people with property are "more responsible, more educated, more knowledgeable, more worthy of confidence" than are those without means, and that the "nation would be better managed if the franchise were restricted to such citizens."[29]

By rejecting these reasons as not just elitist but also constitutionally insufficient, the *Harper* majority made clear that the Court was willing to harness the Equal Protection Clause to more closely scrutinize restrictions on the right to vote, even when those restrictions came in the form of nondiscriminatory and generally applicable laws. Under *Harper*, laws imposing restrictions unrelated to voter qualifications are unconstitutional under the fundamental rights prong of Equal Protection Clause doctrine.

But that only takes us so far. *Harper* applies when the challenged voting restriction is irrelevant to a voter's qualifications. It says little about how to evaluate the constitutionality of laws that *are* relevant to voting qualifications but that *also* burden some people's right to vote more than others. How to evaluate those laws is the question the Court would wrestle with in the next blockbuster voting rights case on our list: *Bush v. Gore.*

The 2000 presidential election was one of the closest in U.S. history. The sitting vice president, Democrat Al Gore, won the nationwide popular vote, but the Electoral College winner, and therefore the winner of the presidency, hinged on whether Gore or the Texas governor, Republican George W. Bush, would win Florida's twenty-five electoral votes. The vote count in Florida was astonishingly close. On election night, Bush led Gore by fewer than 1,800 of the almost six million votes cast in the state.[30] Under Florida law, that triggered an automatic machine recount, which brought the margin down to fewer than 900 votes. Bush was still in the lead, but the gap was closing.[31]

With the presidency hanging in the balance, Gore decided to ask for a manual recount in counties that had a high "undercount."[32] An undercounted ballot is one that records a vote for down-ticket races but fails to record a vote in the presidential race.[33] This was before touchscreen voting machines became common, and many counties in Florida, especially less wealthy and Democratic-leaning counties, used punch card or Scantron (bubble sheet) ballots.[34] These types of ballots can be hard for machines to read. If the voter makes minor errors, like not completely punching through the ballot with their stylus or only incompletely filling in the circle with their No. 2 pencil, the machine may not count the vote (anyone who has taken or graded a Scantron exam can probably relate to this). Manual recounts, like the ones requested by Gore, can correct for that by allowing a human being to count votes the machines miss. Since it is unusual that a person would come to the polls in a presidential election year but choose to not vote in the presidential race, Gore hoped a manual recount of the undervoted ballots would uncover enough additional votes to put him ahead of Bush.

Under Florida law, a vote would be counted during a manual recount if the "clear intent of the voter" could be ascertained from the ballot.[35] Intent standards are common in law, and many state election laws had "intent of the voter" standards similar to Florida's.[36] Such standards may sound subjective but often work quite well. For years, I have shown students images of actual ballots from the Florida election. After reviewing the ballots, they tend to agree on whether a given ballot evidences a voter's intent to vote for a candidate, and if so, which one. For example, on a Scantron ballot a voter will do things like fill in one bubble, then cross out that bubble and fill in a different one, sometimes including an arrow pointing to the uncrossed-out/filled-in bubble. A machine could not read this ballot, but my students have little difficulty understanding and agreeing on what the voter was trying to convey. Under Florida's intent of the voter standard, a vote like this was a legal vote and could be counted in a manual recount.

But in the intense spotlight of a highly consequential and shockingly close election (Florida ended up being decided by a margin of just 0.009 percent; 537 of 5,963,100 votes cast[37]), county canvassing boards conducting the recount were under tremendous pressure to develop more specific rules to define the intent of the voter standard. The Florida Supreme Court, which by this point was overseeing the recount, had reiterated that standard but had not provided guidance about how to implement it statewide.[38] So county canvassing boards began making their own rules.[39] These rules specified things like how many sides of an octagonal hole punch had to be perforated for a vote to show the voter's intent, whether partially detached perforations counted, and how many stray marks on a bubble sheet it took to disqualify a Scantron ballot.[40]

The problem was that these rules were different in different counties. In some cases, the rules were even changed within a county as the count went on.[41] With Gore gaining ground as more votes were counted, Bush seized on those differences to file an emergency petition with the Supreme Court asking the Court to stop the recount. The basis of his claim was the Equal Protection Clause. His argument was that counting votes using different standards in different counties violated Equal Protection because a voter in one county might not have their vote counted under the canvassing rules used by that county even though an identical ballot cast by a voter in a different county using different canvassing rules would be counted. There was no justification, Bush argued, for this disparate treatment of similarly situated voters.[42]

That seems like a reasonable argument, and seven of the nine justices ultimately accepted some version of it (the famous 5–4 split in the case was not on the equal protection claim, but on whether the recount should be stopped entirely or remanded to the Florida Supreme Court to develop a more uniform counting process).[43] But it was not at all obvious at the time that the Court would intervene, or that Bush's argument would prevail if they did. The conservative justices who dominated the Court tended to be skeptical of these types of equal protection claims. After all, there was no suspect class at issue in the case, and no accusation (by Bush) that either the State of Florida or the county canvassing boards had enacted or applied their rules in an intentionally discriminatory way. It seemed unlikely that a conservative Court with a strong "state's rights" bent would for the first time expand equal protection this way to interfere in a state's election administration in the midst of a hotly contested presidential election.

Even more fundamentally, the justices had never before applied federal constitutional law to the type of routine administrative rules and regulations Bush was challenging. Prior to *Bush v. Gore*, the Court had applied the fundamental rights prong of equal protection doctrine to state-level policy choices, such as laws involving poll taxes (*Harper*) and legislative districting (*Reynolds v. Sims*).[44] What was new in *Bush* was the Court's decision to apply that doctrine to the type of technical rules at issue in that case—things governing the mechanics of how to cast and count legal ballots under state law. As we have seen, the choices made by election administrators routinely create differences in how votes are cast and counted, both within and between states. Indeed, this was obvious in *Bush* itself: The punch card machines used in several Florida counties had significantly higher error rates than machines used in other counties, meaning voters in those counties were less likely to have their votes counted than voters in other parts of the state.[45] If it was unconstitutional for county canvassing boards to use different rules when counting ballots, shouldn't differences like that be unconstitutional as well?

The Court's decision in *Bush v. Gore* anticipated but did not really answer this question. Instead, the five-justice majority wrote this: "Our consideration is limited to the present circumstances, for the problem of equal protection in election processes generally presents many complexities."[46] To most election law scholars, this was an unsatisfying answer. One of the foundational principles of the rule of law is that like things should be treated alike, which means a basic duty of judges is to explain to the rest of us why they have concluded that one thing is like or unlike another, in a legally meaningful way. That is not always easy, and we may not always be convinced by their reasons, but it is a fundamental part of the job for judges to provide them. The problem in *Bush v. Gore* is that the Court barely tried to explain itself. It noted the unusual circumstances of a statewide recount held under the purview of a single judicial body (the Florida Supreme Court) but didn't tell us why that was a constitutionally relevant fact, or what other situations the new rule might apply to.

Nonetheless, *Bush v. Gore* signaled that the Court now stood ready to insert itself into more granular issues of election administration than it had engaged with in the past. Voting rights lawyers took note and immediately went to work challenging other nuts-and-bolts election rules that resulted in similarly situated votes being treated differently. Equal protection arguments were made against differences in the type of voting machines used, the procedures used to validate provisional ballots, the forms of voter identification required to register or vote, the time provided for early or absentee voting, and the treatment of ballots cast at the right polling place but for the wrong precinct.[47] For the most part, these challenges were unsuccessful. Despite the optimism of some voting rights advocates, *Bush v. Gore* proved to be a bit of a dead end, legally speaking.[48] But even as *Bush v. Gore* was floundering in the lower courts, a different way of challenging election laws was emerging out of Indiana.

———

The 2000 election unleashed what one election law scholar has coined "the voting wars."[49] The jarring reminder that the presidency could be won or lost on the basis of a few hundred votes in a single state, and that the courts might well be the final arbitrator of how those votes were cast and counted, fueled an explosion of election-related litigation.[50] To resolve these cases, courts have turned to the doctrine developed in our final case, *Crawford v. Marion County Election Board*.[51]

Crawford involved a photo ID law enacted in Indiana in 2005.[52] States have long required voters to identify themselves at the polls but historically have allowed them to do so in a variety of ways, such as signing poll books, showing utility bills affirming their name and address, or presenting student IDs or social security cards.[53] After the 2000 election, states began passing laws limiting these options. Virtually all of these laws were enacted on a partisan basis. Republicans claimed that stricter ID laws were necessary to prevent voter fraud and supported them, while Democrats argued that they needlessly burdened or disenfranchised marginalized citizens and opposed them.[54]

Indiana's law was fairly exacting for the era.[55] It required in-person voters to present a current (unexpired or recently expired) government-issued photo ID. The name on the ID had to match the name on the voter registration record. People with religious objections to being photographed could cast a provisional ballot, which would be counted only if they completed an affidavit within ten days at the county clerk's office. People without a qualifying ID could receive a voter ID card free of charge, but only by presenting a birth certificate, certificate of naturalization, veteran or military ID, or passport. Obtaining copies of these documents often required paying a fee, so while the voter ID card itself was free, the process of getting one was not. Also, like the affidavit option for religious objectors, obtaining a free voter ID card required at least one trip to the county clerk's office to present the required documents, often in geographically large counties lacking public transportation.[56]

The question presented to the Court in *Crawford* was whether this law violated the Equal Protection Clause. The law treated voters differently, in that voters with a qualifying ID could vote but those without one could not. But it did not intentionally discriminate against a suspect class, so strict scrutiny was not triggered on that basis. *Harper* also was not directly applicable, because state laws requiring voters to identify themselves are not unrelated to voter qualifications; they are a way to enforce the valid qualifications of identity and residency. In addition, courts had not (and have not) extended *Harper*'s prohibition on poll taxes to the other types of costs incurred by voters, such as those required to get identifying documents like birth certificates and passports. *Bush v. Gore* had shown that rules like these could raise viable Equal Protection claims but had given little guidance about how to evaluate such claims in future cases. So what test would the Court use to determine the constitutionality of burdensome but non-discriminatory election laws?

The Court's answer was something called the *Anderson-Burdick* test. This test grew out of two Supreme Court cases, *Anderson v. Celebrezze*[57] and *Burdick v. Takushi*.[58] Generally speaking, the test divides generally applicable, nondiscriminatory voting rules into three categories, based on the burdensomeness of the law. Laws that *severely* burden the right to vote are subject to strict scrutiny review, meaning they must be narrowly tailored to advance a compelling interest. This is true even when the law is not intentionally discriminatory against a suspect class, making it essentially an alternative route to strict scrutiny review for severely burdensome laws. In contrast, laws that impose only de minimis (minor) burdens usually can be justified by a state's important regulatory interests. This means that most laws imposing inconsequential burdens will be quickly and routinely upheld, avoiding excessive judicial oversight of the routine work of election administrators. Finally, all other laws—those whose burdens are neither severe nor de minimis—are subject to a flexible standard of review requiring the state to prove that the "character and magnitude" of the burden is justified by the "precise interests" put forward by the state to justify the rule.[59]

Indiana's photo ID law fell into the third category, which required the justices to balance the state's claimed need for the law against the burdens the law imposed on voters. Applying this test in *Crawford*, the Court upheld the law. Justice John Paul Stevens wrote the lead opinion.[60] He began by considering the state's asserted interests in enacting the law. Indiana argued that the law was necessary to prevent voter fraud and safeguard voter confidence in the electoral process. All of the justices readily agreed that these are valid and important interests. What they disagreed about was whether the purported benefits of the law justified the burdens it imposed.

The problem was that in-person voter impersonation fraud, the only kind Indiana's photo ID law would prevent, is extremely rare. The parties had not identified a single case of any such fraud in Indiana, and only a handful of cases anywhere at any time in U.S. history.[61] That isn't surprising. In-person voter impersonation fraud is a silly way to try to steal an election. Doing it at any scale would require a host of co-conspirators willing to risk criminal penalties by showing up hundreds of times at polling places across the state, armed with the names of registered voters who had not already voted and hoping that no one would question whatever documents or signatures the fraudsters presented.[62] Indiana argued that the bloated nature of its own voting rolls at the time (a problem only Indiana itself could fix) made this type of fraud more possible than it

might otherwise be, but the hard fact was there was scant evidence showing that the law was aimed at solving any actual problem.[63]

Perhaps in tacit recognition of this, Indiana leaned heavily on its
second asserted interest: protecting voter confidence in the integrity of
the election system. This interest, the state argued, is important even
in the absence of actual fraud because democracy doesn't work if voters
think the system is rigged. That's true and the justices again readily
agreed, even though the state had not produced evidence that the law
in fact enhanced voter confidence.[64] (Subsequent research shows that the
effect of such laws is mixed.[65]) But the *Anderson-Burdick* test requires not
just that the state interests in the challenged law be valid but also that
the burdens imposed by the law be proportionate to those interests. Even
when they don't in the end prevent people from voting, laws like this do
impose burdens on the right to vote, and those burdens are rarely evenly
distributed across the population. So Justice Stevens turned next to an
evaluation of those burdens.

Here too, though, the evidence was lacking. The challengers had produced several prospective voters representative of the types of people who
would be unlikely to have qualifying identification and difficulty access-
ing or affording the documents necessary to obtain the free voter ID.[66]
These included elderly people born out of state, lower-income people, and
unhoused people, all of whom the challengers argued would have more
difficulty than others in meeting the requirements of Indiana's law. But the
challengers did not provide reliable information about how many Indiana
voters fit into each of these categories or concrete evidence of the burden
imposed on the specific voters who gave evidence in the case.[67] As Justice
Stevens wrote, the record created in the case said virtually nothing about
the difficulties actually faced by the voters most affected by the law.[68]

So in the end the Court was stuck with balancing a law that didn't
really seem necessary against a burden that didn't really seem that high.
In that scenario, Justice Stevens tipped the scales in favor of deferring
to the judgment of the Indiana state legislature. While leaving the door
open to more targeted challenges better documenting the burdens im-

posed by the law, Stevens held that based on the record presented, the limited burden imposed on the voters' rights was sufficiently justified by the state's interests.[69]

Together, *Crawford*, *Bush*, and *Harper* allow us to think comprehensively about the types of claims considered in both this chapter and the previous one. As we have learned, there are multiple ways that rules burdening voting rights can be challenged under the Equal Protection Clause. Burdens that are intentionally discriminatory against a suspect class will be subject to strict scrutiny review under the Fourteenth or Fifteenth Amendments and will only be constitutional when narrowly tailored to advance a compelling state interest. Under *Harper*, burdens (like poll taxes) that are arbitrary or otherwise unrelated to voter qualifications also are likely to be unconstitutional under the Equal Protection Clause. But other laws, generally applicable laws that are nondiscriminatory (in the constitutional sense), are subject to the *Anderson-Burdick* test. Under that test, laws imposing severe burdens must pass strict scrutiny and will usually be invalidated, while laws imposing minor burdens receive minimal judicial review and will usually be upheld. When the burden falls between these extremes, like Indiana's photo ID law, states must demonstrate that the burden is justified relative to the need.

The *Anderson-Burdick* test is a pragmatic approach to the question posed at the start of this chapter about how courts should evaluate nondiscriminatory laws burdening the right to vote. In theory, it puts states to their proof regarding the need for such laws, while avoiding excessive judicial second-guessing of how election administrators manage the day-to-day administration of the nation's electoral systems. Nonetheless, *Anderson-Burdick* has been subject to criticism. It is essentially a balancing test, and balancing tests give quite a bit of discretion to judges. This is especially so in *Anderson-Burdick* in regard the critical question of the severity of the burden imposed by a challenged law. What seems severe to one judge may seem merely inconvenient to another.

The more pressing concern, though, has been the willingness of judges to accept at face value claims made by states about the need for their laws. This has been true even when, unlike in *Crawford*, challengers have presented ample evidence of the burden imposed on some of the most vulnerable members of our society.[70] Since widespread allegations of massive voter fraud in recent presidential elections, dozens of states have enacted more and more burdensome laws in the name of protecting election security. According to the Brennan Center for Justice, voters in more than half of the states face new barriers to voting enacted since 2020.[71] These include laws restricting who can return completed absentee ballots on behalf of other voters,[72] imposing criminal penalties on election workers who make minor errors,[73] limiting the assistance that voters can receive at the polls,[74] and disqualifying ballots for inconsequential errors.[75] More recently, President Trump signed an executive order, sure to be challenged in court, instructing the Election Assistance Commission to revise the federal voter registration form (discussed in Chapter 4) to require documentary proof of citizenship nationwide, to prohibit states from counting ballots received after election day regardless of when they were mailed, and to require federal review of state voter registration datasets for compliance with these and other applicable federal laws.[76]

Virtually all of these laws and regulations are adopted on a purely partisan basis, and many of them have serious impacts on the voters required to navigate them.[77] While the burdens they impose may not be as egregious as the Louisiana literacy test, they are the latest iteration of a long history in our country of stoking fears of voter fraud to justify making it harder for some Americans to vote. Yet courts have for the most part failed to invalidate them under the *Anderson-Burdick* test.[78] Instead, judges have read *Crawford* as instructing them to defer in most cases to legislative assertions about the need to protect voter confidence and election integrity.

All of which has led voting rights advocates to look for different solutions.

State constitutions are one option. Unlike the U.S. Constitution, virtually all our state constitutions include explicit textual provisions protecting a general right to vote.[79] Advocates have used those provisions with varying success to fill the gaps left by federal law.[80] But state-specific remedies, even at their best, will leave the voting rights of some Americans at risk. That's why Richard Hasen, a prominent election law scholar, has proposed a federal Right to Vote Amendment.[81] As we saw in the last chapter, amending the U.S. Constitution to protect an affirmative right to vote is not a new idea, but Hasen's proposal is notable in its detailed effort to resolve some of the most troubling vulnerabilities of our current system.

Hasen's basic version (he offers several) of a proposed amendment gives all adult, resident, nonfelon American citizens an affirmative right to vote in all elections held in their jurisdiction. It also puts teeth in the *Anderson-Burdick* test by prohibiting states from unduly burdening voting rights without "substantial reasons" backed by "real and significant evidence," and makes clear that Congress has broad power to enact federal laws protecting the right to vote.[82] Hasen's more ambitious version of the amendment also constitutionalizes several of the protections discussed in this book, including the one-person, one-vote rule of *Reynolds* and Section 2 of the Voting Rights Act.[83]

As Hasen is well aware, passing constitutional amendments is challenging, and would be especially so in our highly polarized political environment. But few things are as important in a self-governing society as the right to vote. After all, as the Supreme Court itself has recognized, the right to vote is fundamental not because it ensures the best outcomes but because it is preservative of all our other rights.[84] It is the most basic way that each and every one of us is empowered to have an equal say in how we are governed and the rules under which we will live. Generations of Americans have understood this and have fought for their right to vote and to have their vote counted. How we, the voters of today, might continue that fight is the topic we will turn to next.

Conclusion

We the Voters

Is it not the glory of the people of America that, whilst they
have paid a decent regard to the opinions of former times
and other nations, they have not suffered a blind veneration for antiquity, for custom, or for names, to overrule the
suggestions of their own good sense, the knowledge of their
own situation, and the lessons of their own experience?

—JAMES MADISON, Federalist 14, 1788

In a large and diverse country like the United States, people will disagree about many things, including how we govern ourselves. These
disagreements can be disingenuously manufactured in bad faith or for
personal gain, but they also can be well-informed, deep, and sincere.
The purpose of a well-functioning system of democratic self-government
is not to permanently resolve such differences or to pretend they do not
exist, but rather to provide a reliable, fair, and representative framework
through which we work through them, together. The convoluted, mallea-
ble, imperfect, persistent democratic republic we share today is the result
of past struggles to build that framework and, when it wasn't working, to
change it.

As we have seen throughout this book, Americans have done just
that many, many times. The unity of the Revolutionary War gave way

to bickering among the states about the system of government set up in the Articles of Confederation. The compromises made by the authors of the 1787 Constitution to change that system gave us a stronger union but also gave white southerners disproportionate power, created an unworkable scheme for electing the president, and failed to prevent the nation's descent into civil war. The Reconstruction Amendments enacted in the wake of that war held out the promise of a more inclusive democracy but did little to protect the embryonic multiracial governments emerging in southern states after the war. Instead, these amendments essentially sat dormant until they were finally given new life by Congress and the courts almost a century later. Through state and federal laws, judicial decisions, and constitutional amendments, prior generations of Americans have changed how we elect the president, the way we distribute representation and political power, who gets access to the ballot, and whether the states or the federal government have the final say over the rules governing our electoral systems.

These earlier disputes about American self-government raised fundamental questions about how democracy in America should work. Our disputes today, over things like the growing anti-majoritarianism of the U.S. Senate, the allocation of power in state legislatures, and the perpetually unpopular Electoral College system, are different than the battles fought by prior generations of Americans, but those fundamental questions—who "we the people" are, how they should be represented, and who makes the rules—remain the same.

Like our predecessors, we should not be afraid to think critically about those questions, and, when necessary, to change what isn't working. After all, as James Madison said, the "glory" of the people of America is that we are *not* bound by veneration of the past but free to use lessons learned from our own experience to change things. Madison and the other men who wrote the 1787 Constitution did exactly that, by building on their deep knowledge of other forms of government to design our governing institutions to enable the elaborate system of checks and balances and separation of powers that are the basic building blocks of our democratic republic. The authors and ratifiers of the Reconstruction Amendments then used the hard-learned lessons of the Civil War to rebuild and restructure those institutions in the wake of that war, and generations of judges, elected leaders, and ordinary Americans have used their lived experiences ever since to realize and expand on that more inclusive and equitable vision of what democracy in America could be.

These generations of Americans have left their mark on how our system of self-government works, and so can we.

The most straightforward way to do that is also the easiest: If you are able, vote. Without voting, no other form of democratic change is possible. Your individual vote may not feel like much, but our votes together shape the coalitions that elect our leaders and determine our legislative majorities. That makes voting the critical foundation of the Madisonian system of competing institutions of government, each responsive in different ways to different voters at different times, checking and balancing each other. Which is why Americans have long understood that protecting our interests requires casting our ballots.

Every year, millions of Americans do just that by registering to vote. They avow their citizenship under penalty of perjury. They provide identification when registering, the first time they show up to vote, or both. States check those registrations against other datasets, remove ineligible and inactive voters at regular intervals, and take additional steps to ensure that the state's registration rolls are as accurate as they can be while avoiding removing voters by mistake or without notice. Once registered, voters then cast their ballots in any one of the myriad ways permitted by different states and localities. Some vote by mail. Others take advantage of early in-person voting. And, of course, millions of us choose to share the moment with our fellow Americans on election day itself by showing up to cast ballots in person at our local precincts.

As we learned in Chapter 4, though, voting is just the first step in a complex process of administering our elections. Behind the scenes, thousands of election officials across the country work hard to keep our elections safe and secure. Ballots are counted and tracked from the time

145

they are printed to when they are bundled up and archived. Local election officials use established chain-of-custody procedures to ensure that ballots are accounted for and tabulated correctly. Mailed-in ballots are processed and counted, machine tallies are recorded and audited, and, in close elections, everything is recounted and re-audited even more extensively. Election observers witness virtually all aspects of this process, and courts use pre-established state contest procedures to hear and resolve challenges. Then, at the end of this process, we have a new set of leaders, chosen by us, the American voters. They may not be the ones you wanted, but democracy requires being willing not just to fight but also to lose.

While voting is essential to making our democracy work, as we have seen throughout this book it isn't the only way engaged Americans throughout history have changed our system of self-government. People also can, and do, advocate directly for more systemic changes. There are a host of local, state, and federal laws structuring our system of self-government. By better understanding what those laws are, who makes them, and who has the power to change them, you can engage in democratic action not just by voting but also by talking to your neighbors, making your opinions known to our leaders, and otherwise advocating for the changes you want to see.

That can involve working with local, state, or even federal officials. Most nuts-and-bolts election administration rules are made at the state or local level, by state legislatures, county boards, or local election officials. So if you want more polling locations, instant runoff voting, or different ways of casting your ballot, advocacy directed at those entities is one way to facilitate that type of change. State legislatures also are the institutions where some elected leaders are debating changing how we allocate representation under the "one person, one vote" rule of *Reynolds v. Sims*. Issues like these, because they are made at the state or local level, provide an ideal opportunity to make your voice heard by serving on local boards or commissions, attending their meetings, volunteering at the polls, or even just calling your state or local representatives to register your opinion on the questions of the day.

Legislative districting—the line drawing that determines how we distribute representation—also is done mainly by state legislatures. But as we saw in *Arizona State Legislature v. Arizona Independent Redistricting Commission*, citizens who live in states permitting lawmaking by popular referendum can use those procedures to push or even require states to adopt districting schemes less subject to partisan gerrymandering and other forms of political manipulations. Understanding the law in your state and who has the power to change it empowers you to take more informed action on issues like these.

State legislatures also draw the legislative boundaries for the state's congressional districts. Here, though, Congress can play more of a role by exercising its power to regulate the "times, places, and manner" of congressional elections. Congress almost certainly, for example, could enact federal legislation limiting partisan gerrymandering of congressional districts, or otherwise regulating congressional elections to limit burdens on voting rights and ensure fair representation. Currently, federal law requires states to create single-member congressional districts, but there is no other federal or constitutional restriction on the ability of states to experiment with drawing congressional districts that elect multiple members per district or distribute representation based on the percentage of the vote a given political party wins in the state. So repealing the single-member district rule could open up a host of opportunities for state experimentation about how members of the House of Representatives are elected. States also, of course, could experiment right now with these alternative districting methods when drawing their state legislative districts, through either state-level legislation or amendments to state constitutions.

Changing how we elect the president, in contrast, may well require amending the U.S. Constitution. As discussed in Chapter 3, the existing Electoral College process could be tweaked by state legislative changes to state laws, such as authorizing the state to sign the National Popular Vote Compact or enacting state laws adopting district-based or proportionate allocation of a state's electoral votes. But these modifications, as we saw, present their own challenges: There are limits to our ability to legislate our way out of the basic Electoral College structure embedded in the Constitution. This means that securing lasting changes in how we elect our president almost certainly requires amending the Constitution. Guaranteeing that all American citizens have a clear and unequivocal constitutional right to vote unhindered by needless barriers, as envisioned by the Right to Vote Amendment discussed in Chapter 6, also would require a constitutional amendment.

Amending the Constitution is not easy, but it is possible. It's a two-step process. First, there's a proposal step. Congress itself can propose an amendment, which requires a vote of two-thirds or better in both chambers. Or Congress can call a convention to consider proposals, when petitioned to do so by the legislatures of at least two-thirds of the states. Then, regardless of which method is used to initiate the process, there's a ratification step. To approve a proposed amendment, at least three-fourths of the states have to vote to ratify it, either in the state legislatures or in state conventions called for that purpose (the choice is up to Congress).

Obviously, this is an elaborate and difficult process. Some elements of it—such as proposing amendments through another constitutional convention—have never been used, and there are lively debates about how these untested parts of the process would work and whether triggering them would be wise.[1] And yet we have in fact amended the Constitution twenty-seven times. While not spread out evenly across time, those twenty-seven amendments represent on average more than one amendment for each decade since the Constitution went into effect in 1789. So it is not an impossible task.

Nor is there just one template for how long it should take, or the circumstances under which we should attempt it. The first ten amendments (the Bill of Rights) grew out of the constitutional ratifying conventions held in the states, were proposed by the first Congress, and then ratified by state legislatures. The Twelfth Amendment was written and ratified quickly to fix the particular problem caused under the original Electoral College scheme of having electors cast undifferentiated votes for president and vice president. The Thirteenth, Fourteenth, and Fifteenth Amendments were proposed by the Reconstruction Congress and ratified by the states in relatively quick succession in the wake of the Civil War, and on an overwhelmingly party-line basis. The Twenty-sixth Amendment, constitutionalizing the right of people aged eighteen years and older to vote, was passed when young men drafted to fight in the Vietnam War successfully argued that if they were old enough to fight they were old enough to vote.[2] But voting rights for women had been debated in America for more than a century before finally being constitutionalized in the Nineteenth Amendment in 1920.

Let's pause there for just a moment. We haven't discussed the Nineteenth Amendment in any detail, but it is a good illustration of how amending the Constitution works. Women begin fighting for the right to vote long before 1920. In fact, debates about women's suffrage are as old as the republic. New Jersey permitted unmarried adult property holders, including women, to vote from 1776 through 1807.[3] The gathering in 1848 at Seneca Falls, New York, which was convened to discuss the "social, civil, and religious rights of woman," brought women's suffrage to the forefront of the women's rights movement.[4] That movement, at least for a while, aligned closely with abolitionists and Black leaders like Frederick Douglass to fight for the right of all adults to vote, regardless of race or gender.[5] Leaders of the women's suffrage movement also were active in debates about the scope of the Fifteenth Amendment and worked hard to include sex along with race as a prohibited basis of denying access to the ballot.[6] When those efforts failed, the movement split bitterly over whether to continue to support the amendment without that prohibition, opening a chasm that haunts the women's movement to this day.[7]

Advocates of women's suffrage didn't just lobby Congress, though. They also pushed their cause in a variety of different ways and different

149

places. They argued (unsuccessfully) at the Supreme Court that the Four-teenth Amendment already guaranteed adult women the right to vote as a "privilege or immunity" of citizenship, regardless of whether such a right was included in the Fifteenth Amendment.[8] They also were active at the state and local level, and especially on the western frontier where a host of circumstances created a convergence of interests they could lever-age for their cause.[9] Here, their work paid off. In 1869, the Wyoming territorial legislature granted women the right to vote and hold office. Utah followed, then Washington, Montana, Colorado, and, eventually, a host of other states.[10]

This success at the state and local level eventually had national con-sequences. Members of Congress elected from states that had expanded the franchise now owed their seats in part to the women back home who had voted for them. Women's support of the war effort during World War I, political party competition, and relentless campaigning combined to generate sufficient support in Congress that, finally in 1919, the Nine-teenth Amendment constitutionalizing the right to vote without regard to sex was able to gain the two-thirds support needed in both houses to send the proposed amendment to the states for ratification.[11] All of which led, in August 18, 1920, to a Tennessee representative, anecdotally in response to a plea from his mother, casting the tie-breaking vote to make Tennessee the thirty-sixth and final state needed to add the Nineteenth Amendment to the U.S. Constitution.[12]

Even then, though, the right of women to vote was not fully real-ized. Voting rights for women of color, compromised away by too many white suffragists, would not become a practical reality nationwide until Congress passed the Voting Rights Act decades later. Young women, like young men, would have to wait for ratification of the Twenty-sixth Amendment before they could cast their ballots. And while all states were bound by the Nineteenth Amendment once ratified, many showed their displeasure by refusing to even symbolically ratify the amendment for years. Florida, South Carolina, Georgia, Louisiana and North Carolina didn't ratify until the late 1960s and early 1970s, and Mississippi refused to do so until 1984.[13] Today, legislative efforts to impose more restrictive voter identification requirements may, depending on how they are implemented, pose new barriers to voting for transgender women and married women who change their names.

The point is this: Amending the U.S. Constitution is rarely a short-term project. Even though the Nineteenth Amendment itself was proposed and ratified within fourteen months, advocates of women's suffrage worked for a long time and used a variety of methods to build the support needed to get to that final step. Many of our most meaningful and transformative amendments have been the result of this type of process. They have been the result of decades, not just years, of effort by dedicated and engaged people working together at the local, state, and national levels. Those early efforts sometimes succeed, but they also frequently fail.

All of which illustrates a simple point. If the change you want requires a constitutional amendment, the only way forward is to dig in and work for it. Your efforts won't be perfect and they may not succeed right away, but that doesn't make them not worth doing. After all, as James Madison said in the quote opening this chapter, if our good sense and experience of our own situation—our democracy, as it works today—lead us to want to change it, then that is exactly what we should do.

———

In Danielle Allen's beautiful book about the Declaration of Independence, she drew out the final words of that short text. "We," the signers promised, "mutually pledge to each other our Lives, our Fortunes, and our sacred Honor." With these words, Allen wrote, the men who signed the Declaration and the people on whose behalf they acted pledged everything they had to each other. In her words, they "staked their claim to independence on the bedrock of equality."[14] They were creating a nation of equal citizens out of a group of loosely connected colonists. They were making a people.

Their understanding of who was part of "the people" they were creating was too narrow, and their plans for how those people would govern themselves did not always work. The Revolution succeeded, but the Articles of Confederation failed. The 1787 Constitution has persevered, but only after civil war and twenty-seven amendments (and counting). Yet through all of these fits and starts, one thing held constant. At every step of this ongoing process, change happened because people acted. Since the founding, Americans have debated and fought over virtually every important aspect of how we will govern ourselves. And in doing so, we have listened, learned, organized, and changed.

That is the hard work of "doing" democracy in America. As the signers of the Declaration understood so many generations ago, the idea of an American people is, more than anything else, the promise of a diverse and expanding population to bind themselves together to *become* a people. That is the great American experiment in democratic self-governance, and we owe it to ourselves and each other to not give up on it but instead to find a way forward, together, toward the more perfect union promised by our founders.

NOTES

Introduction

1. John Lewis, "Together, You Can Redeem the Soul of Our Nation," *New York Times*, July 30, 2020, https://www.nytimes.com/2020/07/30/opinion/john-lewis-civil-rights-america.html (published posthumously at his request).

Chapter 1

1. For example, contrast Sanford Levinson, *Our Undemocratic Constitution: Where the Constitution Goes Wrong (And How We the People Can Correct It)* (Oxford University Press, 2006) with Randy Barnett, *Our Republican Constitution: Securing the Liberty and Sovereignty of We the People* (HarperCollins, 2016).

2. For an in-depth discussion of this issue, see Willi Paul Adams, *The First American Constitutions: Republican Ideology and the Making of the State Constitutions in the Revolutionary Era* (University of North Carolina Press, 1980).

3. Akhil Reed Amar, *America's Constitution: A Biography* (Random House, 2005), pp. 276–281 (discussing the various uses of the terms "democracy" and "republic" in the founding era and providing numerous examples of common usages and dictionary definitions showing the overlap between the two terms); Akhil Reed Amar, "Founding Myths," in *Myth America*, edited by Kevin Krise and Julian Zelizer (Basic Books, 2022), p. 26; and Robert W. Shoemaker, "'Democracy' and 'Republic' as Understood in Late Eighteenth-Century America," *American Speech* 41, no. 2 (May 1966): 83, https://www.jstor.org/stable/453126

("John Adams was bothered in 1788 by a 'peculiar sense in which the words re-public, commonwealth [or] popular state [were] used by . . . writers who mean by them a democracy.' He and others who complained about the confused usage of *democracy* and *republic* had ample grounds for doing so, because the terms were used in a variety of ways.") (citing John Adams, *A Defence of the Constitutions of the United States of America* (1794), III, 160–161). Merrill Jensen, writing in 1957, traced the definition of "democracy" back even further, citing a meeting in New-port, Rhode Island, in 1641 equating "democracy" with "popular government" or "the power of the body of freemen, orderly assembled, or the major part of them, to make or constitute just laws, by which they will be regulated, and to depute from among themselves such minsters as shall see them faithfully exe-cuted between man and man." Merrill Jensen, "Democracy and the American Revolution," *Huntington Library Quarterly* 20, no. 4 (August 1957): 324, https://www.jstor.org/stable/3816275.

4. For an examination of this usage, see Gerald Leonard and Saul Cornell, *The Partisan Republic: Democracy, Exclusion, and the Fall of the Founders' Constitu-tion, 1780s–1830s* (Cambridge University Press, 2019), pp. 15–28. Leonard and Cornell's main theme is how the federalist courts, led by Chief Justice John Mar-shall, transformed the Constitution from a political to a legalized document in the early nineteenth century, which they identify as Marshall's "Federalist legal-ism."

5. James Madison uses this definition in Federalist 10, discussed shortly. Leonard and Cornell emphasize both of these later definitions in their work, as well as the relatively little active engagement many of the Federalists expected average citizens to have in the actual work of governing. Leonard and Cornell, *The Partisan Republic*, pp. 2–5 (describing the founders as opposed to "democ-racy" and elaborating on Madison's belief that the political process set up by the 1787 Constitution would deliberately limit the "operational influence of the people" by creating institutional structures that would "modify and refine the raw democratic will of the people"). Leonard and Cornell also emphasize the role of judicial review in limiting unconstrained majoritarianism.

6. Thomas E. Ricks, *First Principles: What America's Founders Learned from the Greeks and Romans and How That Shaped Our Country* (HarperCollins, 2020), pp. 83–84, 119; Pauline Maier, *Ratification: The People Debate the Constitution, 1787–1788* (Simon & Schuster, 2010), p. 289.

7. Amar, "Founding Myths," p. 32. Robert Shoemaker notes that Montes-quieu defined a republic as an umbrella term for any government in which the

people or a part of the people were considered supreme. Thus, a democracy was a subset of a republic, with an aristocracy being another. Robert W. Shoemaker, "'Democracy' and 'Republic' as Understood in Late Eighteenth-Century America," p. 85. This definition is similar to the one Madison uses in Federalist 39, and Montesquieu is known to have been influential on the framers. See Ricks, *First Principles*, pp. 82, 87–90, 193. See also Franita Tolson, "Protecting Political Participation Through the Voter Qualifications Clause of Article I," *Boston College Law Review* 56, no. 1 (January 2015): 191, https://papers.ssrn.com/sol3/papers.cfm?abstract_id=2485924 (discussing ratification debates involving the Republican Form of Government Clause, and noting as "fairly common" in the period Roger Sherman's republican form of government as one "especially denominate[d]" by "its dependence on the public or the people at large, without hereditary powers.") (citing Letter from Roger Sherman to John Adams, July 20, 1789, *The Works of John Adams, Second President of the United States: with a Life of the Author, Notes and Illustrations, by his Grandson Charles Francis Adams*, Vol. 4 (Little, Brown, 1856).

8. Michael Schudson, *The Good Citizen: A History of American Civic Life* (Free Press, 1998), p. 51 ("The founders' political thought spared little time over the obligations or virtues of the general citizenry and labored instead over the details of representation").

9. Akhil Reed Amar, "The Central Meaning of Republican Government: Popular Sovereignty, Majority Rule, and the Denominator Problem," *University of Colorado Law Review* 65, no. 4 (1994): 750, https://heinonline.org/HOL/P?h=hein.journals/ucollr65&i=773.

10. Pauline Maier, *American Scripture: Making the Declaration of Independence* (Knopf, 1997), p. 192 (describing "equality" mentioned in the Declaration of Independence).

11. Judith N. Shklar, *American Citizenship: The Quest for Inclusion* (Harvard University Press, 1995), pp. 33–45 (discussing colonial ideas of suffrage as applying to white, property-owning men).

12. See generally Shklar, *American Citizenship*; Eric Foner, *The Story of American Freedom* (Norton, 1998), p. 39.

13. See, for example, *Kistner v. Simon*, No. A20–1486 (Order, Minnesota Supreme Court, 2020) (seeking temporary restraining order enjoining certification of the November 3 election on the grounds that certain vote-by-mail procedures had been improperly suspended); *Texas Democratic Party v. Abbott*, 961 F.3d 389 (2020) (alleging that a Texas law permitting only individuals age 65 or older to

vote by mail was unconstitutional); *In re: Enforcement of Election Laws and Securing Ballots Cast or Received After 7 pm on November 3, 2020*, No. SPCV20–00982 (Order, Georgia Superior Court, Chatham, 2020) (complaint claiming that the Chatham County Board of Elections in Georgia had failed to safely store absentee ballots); and *Trump v. Degraffenreid*, No. 20–845 (U.S. Supreme Court) (challenging the way the Philadelphia County Board of Elections had configured their ballot-canvassing tables).

14. Maier, *American Scripture*, pp. 152–153. For a rich discussion of the core arguments presented in the Declaration, see Danielle Allen, *Our Declaration: A Reading of the Declaration of Independence in Defense of Equality* (Liveright, 2014). See also Frederick Douglass, "What to the Slave Is the Fourth of July?" (speech, Corinthian Hall, Rochester, New York, 1852).

15. David Armitage discusses the importance of the Declaration's claim that the future Americans were "one people" entitled, collectively, to govern themselves free and distinct from the king and Parliament. See David Armitage, *The Declaration of Independence: A Global History* (Harvard University Press, 2008).

16. Edmund S. Morgan, *Inventing the People: The Rise of Popular Sovereignty in England and America* (Norton, 1988), pp. 123–125 (describing early colonial assemblies).

17. Alan Taylor, *American Revolutions: A Continental History, 1750–1804* (Norton, 2016), pp. 31–38. See also Harry M. Ward, *Colonial America: 1607–1763* (Pearson, 1990), pp. 192–208.

18. An elected body in Virginia had participated in governing the colony since 1618, while New York's assembly dated to 1683. Morgan, *Inventing the People*, pp. 123–125.

19. Morgan, *Inventing the People*, pp. 39–40.

20. Morgan, *Inventing the People*, p. 43; Taylor, *American Revolutions*, pp. 31–35.

21. Bernard Bailyn, *The Ideological Origins of the American Revolution* (Belknap Press, 1967), pp. 189–204. See also James T. Kloppenberg, *Toward Democracy: The Struggle for Self-Rule in European and American Thought* (Oxford University Press, 2016), pp. 303-304.

22. Marc Egnal and Joseph A. Ernst, "An Economic Interpretation of the American Revolution," *William and Mary Quarterly* 29, no. 1 (1972): 7. See also Maier, *American Scripture*, pp. 29–31; Taylor, *American Revolutions*, pp. 52–53.

23. Bailyn, *Ideological Origins*, p. 190. See also Kloppenberg, *Toward Democracy*, pp. 301-303.

24. Robert M. Weir, "Who Shall Rule at Home: The American Revolution as a Crisis of Legitimacy for the Colonial Elite," *Journal of Interdisciplinary History* 6, no. 4 (Spring 1976): 685–695, https://www.jstor.org/stable/pdf/202536.pdf.

25. Weir, "Who Shall Rule at Home," p. 685; Aziz Rana, *The Two Faces of American Freedom* (Harvard University Press, 2010), pp. 43–48, 59–80.

26. See Andrew Roberts, *The Last King of America: The Misunderstood Reign of George III* (Viking, 2021).

27. Weir, "Who Shall Rule at Home," p. 695 ("The Declaration of Independence charged not merely that the actions of the crown had been illegal, but also that they had made good government—in fact, any government—impossible; having dissolved colonial assemblies and having delayed the election of their replacements, royal authorities had exposed the colonies to 'all the dangers of invasion from without, and convulsions within.'").

28. Declaration of Independence.

29. Americans saw these actions as a deliberate assault against liberty and as evidence of the corruption of the British government and the Crown, both in America and in England. Stripping the colonists of self-government, in the common but shockingly unself-aware language of men who lived among actual enslaved people, would be to "enslave" them. Bailyn, *Ideological Origins*, p. 119.

30. Taylor, *American Revolutions*, pp. 123–124.

31. Maier, *American Scripture*, p. 30.

32. For a discussion of the methodical approach taken by the Continental Congresses, see Taylor, *American Revolutions*, pp. 123–155. See also Maier, *American Scripture*, pp. 1–8.

33. Maier, *American Scripture*, pp. 8–9, 30, 38.

34. The First Continental Congress was convened in part because of fears of restless mobs agitating for quicker action. Authorizing officially sanctioned delegates to gather and determine an appropriate course of action was their way to avoid the violence of unconstrained mob rule. Taylor, *American Revolutions*, pp. 123–124. For general discussions of the importance the founding generation put on the use of formal institutions and structural design to channel self-government, see Ricks, *First Principles*, pp. 179–180 (connecting this idea to the influence of Montesquieu on early American political thinkers); Schudson, *The Good Citizen*, p. 89 (discussing the expectation of Madison and Jefferson that public opinion would "find its voice in and through the formal institutions of government"); Leonard and Cornell, *The Partisan Republic*, p. 59 ("Still, few Republican leaders were willing to grant constitutional legitimacy to extralegal violence or accept

that local militias might exercise a constitutional checking function on their own, a prospect that seemed closer to mobocracy than republicanism."). As discussed in Chapter 5, the Reconstruction Amendments enacted after the Civil War further solidified the democratic process through formal institutions as the mechanism through which people exercise their sovereignty, including the right to change their governments.

35. Morgan, *Inventing the People*, p. 60 ("It would not do to encourage the unruly to shelter under an illusion that they were the people. Mere people, however many in number, were not *the* people, and the sovereignty of the people must not be confused with the unauthorized actions of individuals or of crowds or even of organized groups outside Parliament") (discussing evolving notions of "the people" and popular sovereignty).

36. The delegates had a variety of opinions about whether, and how rapidly, to pursue impendence. See generally Kloppenberg, *Toward Democracy*, p. 317; Taylor, *American Revolutions*, pp. 140–141.

37. Maier, *American Scripture*, pp. 25–26.

38. Maier, *American Scripture*, pp. 3–7, 25–26, 41–46.

39. Maier, *American Scripture*, pp. 25–32, 48, 59–61. Many of these town and state assemblies wrote and issued their own "declarations of independence" supporting the decisions of the Continental Congress. Maier, *American Scripture*, pp. 45–50.

40. Taylor, *American Revolutions*, pp. 159–160.

41. Maier, *American Scripture*, pp. 43–45, 68; Taylor, *American Revolutions*, pp. 159–160.

42. Taylor, *American Revolutions*, pp. 100–110.

43. Taylor, *American Revolutions*, pp. 135–139.

44. See generally Van Gosse, *The First Reconstruction: Black Politics in America from the Revolution to the Civil War* (University of North Carolina Press, 2021); see also Taylor, *American Revolutions*, p. 110.

45. See generally Morgan, *Inventing the People*, pp. 55–77.

46. The full phrase used in the Declaration is "We, therefore, the Representatives of the united States of America, in General Congress, Assembled, appealing to the Supreme Judge of the world for the rectitude of our intentions, do, in the Name, and by the Authority of the good People of these Colonies, solemnly publish and declare, That these United Colonies are, and of Right ought to be Free and Independent States."

47. Taylor, *American Revolutions*, p. 4; Jennifer Raten-Rosenhagen, *The Ideas That Made America: A Brief History* (Oxford University Press, 2019), pp. 12, 57.

48. Taylor, *American Revolutions*, p. 18 (explaining Virginia's founding and operation primarily as a tobacco colony).

49. Taylor, *American Revolutions*, p. 18.

50. Alan Taylor, *American Colonies*, (Viking, 2001), pp. 133, 182, 247, 264.

51. Taylor, *American Colonies,* pp. 254–255.

52. Taylor, *American Colonies*, pp. 246–260.

53. Taylor, *American Revolutions*, pp. 21, 253–255.

54. See Ratner-Rosenhagen, *The Ideas that Made America*, pp. 12, 57 ("Just as [colonists] had no deep connection to something called 'America,' they also had no shared set of ideas or beliefs, no shared loyalties, because they had no common nationality, religion, or historical memory"; "America was populated with peoples, but not a people, who, with the exception of the Indians, were all transplants from different parts of Europe, each with their own mother tongues, faith traditions, and cultural sensibilities"). See also Taylor, *American Revolutions*, pp. 13–23; Sanford Levinson, *An Argument Open to All: Reading The Federalist in the Twenty-First Century* (Yale University Press, 2015), p. 13 (discussing the "utter fatuity" of John Jay's declaration to the contrary in Federalist 2).

55. For a general discussion of these issues, see Maier, *American Scripture*, pp. 37–46.

56. Jack Rakove, "The Legacy of the Articles of Confederation," *Publius: The Continuing Legacy of the Articles of Confederation* 12, no. 4 (Autumn 1982): 45–66, https://www.jstor.org/stable/3329662. See also Donald S. Lutz, "The Articles of Confederation as the Background to the Federal Republic," *Publius: The Continuing Legacy of the Articles of Confederation* 20, no. 1 (Winter 1990): 55–70, https://www.jstor.org/stable/3330362; Maier, *American Scripture*, p. 7. See also Maier, *Ratification*, pp. 458–459 (noting that Rhode Island was the last state to ratify the Constitution on May 29, 1790).

57. Michael J. Klarman, *The Framers' Coup: The Making of the United States Constitution* (Oxford University Press, 2016), p. 22. See also Maier, *Ratification*, pp. 91–92. See Jack P. Greene, "The Background of the Articles of Confederation," *Publius: The Continuing Legacy of the Articles of Confederation* 12, no. 4 (Autumn 1982): 15–44, https://www.jstor.org/stable/3329661.

58. See Rakove, "The Legacy of the Articles of Confederation." See also Lutz, "The Articles of Confederation as the Background to the Federal Repub-

lic"; and Greene, "The Background of the Articles of Confederation," pp. 15–44.

59. For a discussion of how supermajority rules hindered governance under the Articles, see Dan T. Coenen, "The Originalist Case Against Congressional Supermajority Voting Rules," *Northwestern University Law Review* 106, no. 3 (Summer 2012): 1123, https://papers.ssrn.com/sol3/papers.cfm?abstract_id=2149078.

60. See generally Rakove, "The Legacy of the Articles of Confederation."

61. See generally Rakove, "The Legacy of the Articles of Confederation."

62. Amar, *America's Constitution*, p. 26; Klarman, *The Framers' Coup*, p. 70.

63. Maier, *Ratification*, pp. 17–18.

64. See generally Klarman, *The Framers' Coup*, ch. 1; Maier, *Ratification*, pp. 11–14.

65. See generally Klarman, *The Framers' Coup*, ch. 1; Maier, *Ratification*, pp. 11–14.

66. After the 1787 Constitution was drafted and sent for ratification, Alexander Hamilton expressed how dire he believed the situation was, predicting that if ratification failed, the nation would experience civil war and the dismemberment of the union, as well as the return of monarchies in some states, and a possible absorption or reunification of others with Britain and Spain. Maier, *Ratification*, pp. 68–69. See also David C. Hendrickson, *Peace Pact: The Lost World of the American Founding* (University Press of Kansas, 2003); Max Edling, *A Revolution in Favor of Government: Origins of the U.S. Constitution and the Making of the American State* (Oxford University Press, 2003).

67. Maier, *Ratification*, p. 21; Klarman, *The Framers' Coup*, pp. 108–112.

68. For a full list of delegates, see Robert A. McGuire, *To Form a More Perfect Union: A New Economic Interpretation of the United States Constitution* (Oxford University Press, 2003), pp. 52–53.

69. Levinson, *An Argument Open to All*, p. 59; Taylor, *American Revolutions*, pp. 374–375.

70. See Amar, "Founding Myths," p. 26.

71. Maier, *Ratification*, pp. 183, 192–98, 206, 256, 298–300.

72. See generally McGuire, *To Form a More Perfect Union*, pp. 51–53.

73. Maier, *Ratification*, pp. 17–18, 93–94, 269–70. See also Ricks, *First Principles*, p. 191 (discussing James Madison letter describing the confederation as "nearing collapse" and noting that it "neither ha[d] nor deserve[d] advocates"); Amar, "Founding Myths," pp. 29–30 (discussing George Washington's letter to

the confederation congress); Morgan, *Inventing the People*, pp. 267–268 (discussing Madison's role in bringing about and shaping this discussion at the Constitutional Convention).

74. Klarman, *The Framers' Coup*, p. 244.

75. Jack N. Rakove, *James Madison and the Creation of the American Republic* (Scott, Foreman/Little, Brown Higher Education, 1990), pp. 44- 45.

76. The architects of the 1787 Constitution probably envisioned some form of judicial review, but the robust use of judicial power to protect individual rights did not take hold in America until the twentieth century. Levinson, *An Argument Open to All*, pp. 5, 178–179 (discussing Federalist 78 and 48). See also Jack N. Rakove, *A Politician Thinking: The Creative Mind of James Madison* (University of Oklahoma Press, 2017), p. 120 (discussing Madison's reluctance to add a Bill of Rights to the 1787 Constitution).

77. Klarman, *The Framers' Coup*, pp. 131–132.

78. Klarman, *The Framers' Coup*, pp. 131–133.

79. Maier, *Ratification*, p. 84.

80. Several of the provisions Madison felt most deeply about were not included in the final draft of the constitution approved at the Convention, including a federal counsel of revisions that would have allowed officers of the federal government to veto state legislation they felt was unwise and a scheme of population proportionate representation in the Senate. Rakove, *A Politician Thinking*, pp. 79–81.

81. David Epstein, *The Political Theory of the Federalist* (University of Chicago Press, 1984), pp. 99–101.

82. Federalist 10.

83. Federalist 10.

84. For a discussion of the founders' understanding of the role of majoritarianism in a republic, see, for example, Dan T. Coenen, *The Story of the Federalist: How Hamilton and Madison Reconceived America* (Twelve Tables Press, 2007), pp. 100–101 (noting that the purpose of the "anti-democratic" aspects of the 1787 Constitution was not to enable minority rule but rather to provide a buffer between elite rulers and public sentiment). For a discussion of Madison's evolving thoughts on the matter, see Jack N. Rakove, *A Politician Thinking*, p. 41 (noting that Madison was skeptical of pure majoritarianism as the standard of ascertaining the public good, but his thinking in 1786 was primarily focused on how to improve majority rule, not how to circumvent it). See also Levinson, *An Argument Open to All*, pp. 79–80 (discussing Federalist 22); and Roberto Gargarella, "Elec-

tions, Republicanism, and the Demands of Democracy: A View from the Americas," in *Comparative Election Law*, edited by James A. Gardner (Elgar, 2022), p. 243 (discussing Thomas Jefferson's understanding that a "republican form of government" meant a "government by its citizens in mass, acting directly and personally, according to rules established by the majority" (citing Thomas Jefferson, *Political Writings*, edited by Joyce Appleby and Terence Ball (Cambridge University Press, 1999) p. 209.). See also Coenen, "The Originalist Case Against Congressional Supermajority Voting Rules," p. 1091; Maier, *Ratification*, pp. 295–312 (discussing how anti-federalists accepted the need to submit to the will of the majority when they lost state ratification votes).

85. French political theorist Baron de Montesquieu, who was well-known to the founders, was the most famous proponent of this idea. See generally Ricks, *First Principle*, pp. 88–90.

86. Federalist 10.

87. Epstein, *The Political Theory of the Federalist*, pp. 99–100.

88. In Federalist 10, Madison also argued that larger districts will enable "better" people to run for office. Each representative district will be larger and therefore will contain more qualified individuals who will run for office (Madison calls them "fit characters"). Being of a more fit temper, these men will be less inclined to capitulate to local prejudices, support misguided policies, or succumb to demagoguery. Epstein, *The Political Theory of the Federalist*, pp. 95–96.

89. Kloppenberg, *Toward Democracy*, pp. 427–432.

90. Epstein, *The Political Theory of the Federalist*, p. 46 (discussing Federalist 51).

91. Rakove, *A Politician Thinking*, pp. 122, 149–151. See Levinson, *An Argument Open to All*, pp. 176–177.

92. His *Federalist Papers* co-author, John Jay, may have disagreed. See Federalist 2.

93. Federalist 51. See also Rakove, *A Politician Thinking*, p. 101; and Levinson, *An Argument Open to All*, p. 194.

94. Amar, *America's Constitution*, pp. 276–281.

95. *McCulloch v. Maryland*, 17 U.S. 316, 415 (1819).

96. The framers knew that their constitution was an imperfect compromise. Rakove, *A Politician Thinking*, p. 66 (describing Madison as stressing the importance of providing a mechanism for constitutional amendment because it would be "indecent" for earlier settlers to preclude later ones from the choice of government under which they live). See also Levinson, *An Argument Open to All*, pp.

135–137 (discussing Federalist 14 and 37 and noting that "Publius" acknowledges in those essays that the 1787 Constitution was a series of compromises and that it was "good enough" to be ratified but it would be up to "future generations, understandings its imperfections, to strive to better it through amendment"); Taylor, *American Revolutions*, pp. 155, 383; Klarman, *The Framers' Coup*, pp. 243–256; and Mary Anne Franks, *The Cult of the Constitution* (Stanford University Press, 2020), p. 202 (citing a Washington letter: "I do not think we are more inspired, have more wisdom, or possess more virtue, than those who will come after us").

Chapter 2

1. *Reynolds v. Sims*, 377 U.S. 533 (1964).

2. See Federalist 22; Federalist 80; Sanford Levinson, *An Argument Open to All: Reading the Federalist in the Twenty-First Century* (Yale University Press, 2015), pp. 78–81 (discussing Federalist 22).

3. See generally Pauline Maier, *Ratification: The People Debate the Constitution, 1787–1788* (Simon & Schuster, 2010), p. 24; Dan T. Coenen, *The Story of the Federalist* (Twelve Tables Press, 2007), p. 96 (discussing Hamilton's acceptance of Madison's "Virginia Plan" in *The Federalist Papers*).

4. David Epstein, *The Political Theory of the Federalist* (University of Chicago Press, 1984), pp. 165–166 (discussing Federalist 37).

5. Maier, *Ratification*, p. 269 (noting that Madison believed all confederations to be "productive of anarchy and confusion" and that a government of states would not be sufficient); see also Akhil Reed Amar, "Founding Myths," in *Myth America*, edited by Kevin Krise and Julian Zelizer (Basic Books, 2022), p. 29; Michael J. Klarman, *The Framers' Coup: The Making of the United States Constitution* (Oxford University Press, 2016), ch. 1.

6. Maier, *Ratification*, p. 24.

7. See Klarman, *The Framers' Coup*, pp. 186-187.

8. Klarman, *The Framers' Coup*, p. 187.

9. Klarman, *The Framers' Coup*, p. 185.

10. Klarman, *The Framers' Coup*, pp. 184–185.

11. Klarman, *The Framers' Coup*, p. 190.

12. Klarman, *The Framers' Coup*, pp. 188–190.

13. Klarman, *The Framers' Coup*, pp. 188–189.

14. Klarman, *The Framers' Coup*, pp. 200–205.

15. Klarman, *The Framers' Coup*, p. 201; see also U.S. Constitution, Article V

(providing for an amendment process of the Constitution, provided that "that no State, without its Consent, shall be deprived of its equal Suffrage in the Senate").

16. Klarman, *The Framer's Coup*, pp. 130–131, 201–202.

17. Jack N. Rakove, "The Great Compromise: Ideas, Interests, and the Politics of Constitution Making," *William and Mary Quarterly* 44 (July 1987), pp. 439, 447–500.

18. Maier, *Ratification*, p. 38.

19. Edmund S. Morgan, *Inventing the People: The Rise of Popular Sovereignty in England and America* (Norton, 1988), p. 274.

20. Klarman, *The Framers' Coup*, p. 170.

21. 2 U.S. §2a.

22. Every state is entitled to a minimum of one House member regardless of population, so there can be some inequality even within this chamber of Congress.

23. Klarman, *The Framers' Coup*, p. 257.

24. Klarman, *The Framers' Coup*, ch. 4.

25. Jennifer Raten-Rosenhagen, *The Ideas That Made America: A Brief History* (Oxford University Press, 2019), pp. 67–68; Klarman, *The Framers' Coup*, 258–268.

26. Klarman, *The Framers' Coup*, pp. 258–259, 264–266.

27. Akhil Reed Amar, *America's Constitution: A Biography* (Random House, 2005), pp. 91–98; see also Klarman, *The Framers' Coup*, pp. 258–259; Gordon S. Wood, *Empire of Liberty: A History of the Early Republic, 1789–1815* (Oxford University Press, 2009), pp. 515–516 (discussing the changing demographics of slavery in the colonies).

28. Klarman, *The Framers' Coup*, pp. 258–259.

29. Marvin R. Zahnizer, *Charles Cotesworth Pinckney: Founding Father* (University of North Carolina Press, 1967), p. 99; Klarman, *The Framers' Coup*, p. 104.

30. University of Maryland Slavery Statistics, https://userpages.umbc.edu/~bouton/History407/SlaveStats.htm.

31. Pinckney was adamant about this. Klarman, *The Framers' Coup*, pp. 281–291.

32. U.S. Constitution, Article I, Section 2, paragraph 3 ("The Number of Representatives shall not exceed one for every thirty Thousand . . .").

33. See generally Amar, "Founding Myths," p. 39.

34. See Klarman, *The Framers' Coup*, pp. 273–274.

NOTES TO CHAPTER 2

35. As New York delegate Gouverneur Morris put it, speaking of enslaved individuals, "Are they men?" If so, "then make them citizens and let them vote. Are they property? Why then is no other property included [in the allocation formula]?" Klarman, *The Framers' Coup*, p. 268.

36. Amar, *America's Constitution*, pp. 90–91. See also Klarman, *The Framers' Coup*, pp. 266–268.

37. Klarman, *The Framers' Coup*, p. 269.

38. Klarman, *The Framers' Coup*, p. 270; see also Jack Rakove, "The Legacy of the Articles of Confederation," *Publius: The Continuing Legacy of the Articles of Confederation* 12, no. 4 (Autumn 1982): 45–66.

39. Klarman, *The Framers' Coup*, pp. 269–270.

40. See, for example, Klarman, *The Framers' Coup*, pp. 274–277.

41. Maier, *Ratification*, p. 465.

42. The committee that came up with the Three-Fifths Compromise also included in the package deal that it reported out to the full delegation the removal of a provision that would have required congressional supermajorities to impose certain types of taxes and protection of the foreign slave trade but only until 1800 (later amended to 1808). These provisions were valuable to the northern states and those southern states with less need to import additional enslaved people, and likely contributed to their willingness to accept the overall package. Klarman, *The Framers' Coup*, pp. 288–289.

43. Amar, *America's Constitution*, pp. 99–98.

44. Amar, *America's Constitution*, p. 351.

45. Levinson, *An Argument Open to All*, pp. 196–199 (discussing Federalist 52).

46. 376 U.S. 1 (1964).

47. 377 U.S. 533 (1964).

48. 376 U.S. 1, 8 (1964); see also p. 42 (Justice Harlan, dissenting).

49. James A. Gardner, "Electoral Systems and Conceptions of Politics," in *Comparative Election Law*, edited by James A. Gardner (Elgar, 2022), pp. 145–147 (describing proportional electoral systems).

50. Gary W. Cox, "Strategic Electoral Choice in Multi-Member Districts: Approval Voting in Practice?," *American Journal of Political Science* 28 (November 1984): 722 (describing approval voting in multi-member districts).

51. Apportionment Act of 1842.

52. Gardner, "Electoral Systems and Conceptions of Politics," pp. 142–145 (describing a winner-take-all electoral system).

53. *Wesberry v. Sanders*, 376 U.S. 1, 2 (1964).

54. Brief for Appellants, 5, *Wesberry* (showing Georgia congressional districts as drawn in 1932).

55. Brief for Appellants, 5–6, *Wesberry* (comparing Georgia congressional districts as drawn in 1932 and 1962).

56. *Wesberry v. Sanders*, 8.

57. *Wesberry v. Sanders*, 2.

58. *Wesberry v. Sanders*, 2.

59. *Wesberry v. Sanders*, 2.

60. See Bertrall L. Ross II, "The Representative Equality Principle: Disaggregating the Equal Protection Intent Standard," *Fordham Law Review* 81, no. 1 (October 2012): 204.

61. Ross, "The Representative Equality Principle," p. 204 (citing Stephen Ansolabehere and James M. Snyder Jr., *The End of Inequality: One Person, One Vote and the Transformation of Politics* (Norton, 2008), p. 38).

62. Ross, "The Representative Equality Principle," p. 204.

63. Ross, "The Representative Equality Principle," p. 204.

64. Ross, "The Representative Equality Principle," p. 204.

65. Ross, "The Representative Equality Principle," pp. 204–205.

66. Ross, "The Representative Equality Principle," p. 204.

67. See U.S. Constitution, Article III, Section 2 ("The judicial Power shall extend to all Cases, in Law and Equity, arising under this Constitution, the Laws of the United States, and Treaties made . . .").

68. *Wesberry v. Sanders*, 24 (Justice Harlan, dissenting).

69. *Wesberry v. Sanders*, 13.

70. *Wesberry v. Sanders*, 7–8.

71. *Wesberry v. Sanders*, 3.

72. *Wesberry v. Sanders*, 4.

73. *Wesberry v. Sanders*, 7–8.

74. *Wesberry v. Sanders*, 8.

75. *Wesberry v. Sanders*, 8.

76. *Wesberry v. Sanders*, 10.

77. *Wesberry v. Sanders*, 10–11.

78. *Wesberry v. Sanders*, 13.

79. *Wesberry v. Sanders*, 14.

80. 377 U.S. 533 (1964).

81. *Reynolds v. Sims*, 377 U.S. 533, 537 (1964).

82. *Reynolds v. Sims*, 537–538.

83. *Reynolds v. Sims*, 537–538.

84. *Reynolds v. Sims*, 545–546.

85. U.S. Constitution, Article VI, paragraph 2 ("This Constitution . . . shall be the supreme Law of the Land").

86. For a discussion of the Reconstruction Amendments, see Travis Crum, "Reconstructing Racially Polarized Voting," *Duke Law Journal* 70, no. 2 (November 2020): 261.

87. *Reynolds v. Sims*, 377 U.S. 533, 561–562 (1964).

88. *Crawford v. Marion County Election Board*, 553 U.S. 181 (2008) (state's interests, like preventing voter fraud, were "sufficiently weighty to justify" the limitation on voting rights). Voting as a fundamental right is discussed in Chapter 6.

89. *Yick Wo v. Hopkins*, 118 U.S. 356, 370 (1886).

90. *Yick Wo v. Hopkins*, 370 ("Though not regarded strictly as a natural right, but as a privilege merely conceded by society, according to its will, under certain conditions, nevertheless [the right to vote] is regarded as a fundamental political right, because preservative of all rights").

91. *Reynolds v. Sims*, 561–562 (1964).

92. *Reynolds v. Sims*, 563–565.

93. *Reynolds v. Sims*, 565.

94. As we will see in the next chapter, this reasoning also is in tension with the Electoral College used to elect the president.

95. *Reynolds v. Sims*, 575–575.

96. *Reynolds v. Sims*, 562–563.

97. *Hunter v. City of Pittsburgh*, 207 U.S. 161, 178–179 (1907) ("Municipal corporations are political subdivisions of the state, created as convenient agencies for exercising such of the governmental powers of the state as may be intrusted to them").

98. *Reynolds v. Sims*, 575–576.

99. See Joseph Fishkin, "Weightless Votes," *Yale Law Journal*, 121 (May 2012): 1888.

100. Sanford Levinson has written at length about the Court's refusal to grapple with the substantive question of representation presented but not resolved in cases like *Wesberry* and *Reynolds*. See Sanford Levinson, "One Person, One Vote: A Mantra in Need of Meaning," *North Carolina Law Review* 80, no. 4 (May 2002): 1269.

101. 578 U.S. 54 (2016).

102. *Evenwel v. Abbott*, 578 U.S. 54, 72–74 (2016).

103. *Evenwel v. Abbott*, 74.

104. *Evenwel v. Abbott*, 62. See also Joseph Fishkin, "Taking Virtual Representation Seriously," *William and Mary Law Review* 59, no. 5 (April 2018): 1684.

105. According to a study by one political scientist, it is always possible to draw districts that are roughly equal in both total population and total citizen voting-age population, although at the steep price of diluting the voting power of racial minorities. See Paul H. Edelman, "Evenwel, Voting Power and Dual Districting," *Journal of Legal Studies* 45, no. 1 (January 2016): 203.

106. For a discussion of the benefits of representational versus voter equality, see *Garza v. County of Los Angeles*, 918 F.2d 763 (9th Cir. 1990). Basically, representational equality helps ensure that all people (including voters) have an equal ability to access and try to influence their representatives, because the representatives will be serving the same number of constituents. Voter equality helps ensure that all voters have equal political power in choosing their representatives, because votes across districts carry equal weight in determining who is elected.

107. The exception had been Hawaii. In *Burns v. Richardson*, the U.S. Supreme Court allowed Hawaii to equalize resident voting population rather than total population but did so, in part, because the resulting districting scheme remained very close to having total population equality as well. 384 U.S. 73 (1966).

108. For a discussion of the information collected by the census, and the efforts of the Trump administration to include a citizenship question to enable alternative districting models, see Justin Levitt, "Citizenship and the Census," *Columbia Law Review* 119, no. 5 (June 2019): 1355.

109. See Levinson, *An Argument Open to All*, pp. 203–205.

110. Section 1 of the Fourteenth Amendment protects the "privileges or immunities" of "citizens," but prohibits states from depriving "any person" within its jurisdiction of equal protection of the laws.

111. *Evenwel v. Abbott*, 71.

112. *Evenwel v. Abbott*, 62.

113. *Evenwel v. Abbott*, 73–74.

114. See, for example, Ming Hsu Chen, "The Political (Mis)Representation of Immigrants in the Census," *New York University Law Review* 96, no. 4 (October 2021): 901; Jeff Zalesin, "Beyond the Adjustment Wars: Dealing with Uncertainty and Bias in Redistricting Data," *Yale Law Journal Forum* 130 (October 2020): 186.

115. "Little Federal Model NC Edition," North Carolina House Bill no. 376 (2023); see also Yevgeniy P. Pislar, "Little Federal Model: One County, One Vote," *University of the Pacific Law Review* 53, no. 1 (January 2021): 269.

116. Steven Levitsky and Daniel Ziblatt, *Tyranny of the Minority: Why American Democracy Reached the Breaking Point* (Crown, 2023), pp. 169-170.

117. This is further aggravated in the House, because the Constitution guarantees Wyoming at least one House seat even though its population of about 560,000 is well below the 750,000 that is the current norm for other districts. And then it gets magnified again in the Electoral College (Chapter 3), which awards states representation based on their total congressional delegation—their number of House and Senate members combined.

Chapter 3

1. *Ray v. Blair*, 343 U.S. 214, 228 (1952).

2. For a full discussion of the importance of this moment, see Steven Levitsky and Daniel Ziblatt, *Tyranny of the Minority: Why American Democracy Reached the Breaking Point* (Crown, 2023), pp. 15–20.

3. Jefferson's party also is at times referred to as "Republican" but is distinct from the modern Republican Party, which traces its roots to the era more immediately before the Civil War. See Daniel Walker Howe, *What Hath God Wrought: The Transformation of America, 1815–1848* (Oxford University Press, 2007).

4. Gordon Wood, *Empire of Liberty: A History of the Early Republic, 1789–1815*, 2nd ed. (Legal Classics Library, 2014), pp. 154, 162; Gerald Leonard and Saul Cornell, *The Partisan Republic: Democracy, Exclusion, and the Fall of the Founders' Constitution, 1780s–1830s* (Cambridge University Press, 2019), pp. 78–79.

5. Michael Schudson, *The Good Citizen: A History of American Civic Life* (Free Press, 1998), p. 111; Thomas E. Ricks, *First Principles: What America's Founders Learned from the Greeks and Romans and How That Shaped Our Country* (Harper-Collins, 2020), p. 222.

6. Wood, *Empire of Liberty*, p. 140. See also James T. Kloppenberg, *Toward Democracy: The Struggle for Self-Rule in European and American Thought* (Oxford University Press, 2016), pp. 203–204; Ricks, *First Principles*, p. 222; Schudson, *The Good Citizen*, p. 111.

7. Wood, *Empire of Liberty*, pp. 276–278.

8. Wood, *Empire of Liberty*, p. 283.

9. William Josephson and Beverly J. Ross, "Repairing the Electoral College,"

Journal of Legislation 22, no. 2 (1996): 154; Leonard and Cornell, *The Partisan Republic*, p. 81; Wood, *Empire of Liberty*, pp. 284–285.

10. Steven Levitsky and Daniel Ziblatt, *Tyranny of the Minority: Why American Democracy Reached the Breaking Point* (Crown, 2023), pp. 18–19; Edward B. Foley, *Presidential Elections and Majority Rule: The Rise, Demise, and Potential Restoration of the Jeffersonian Electoral College* (Oxford University Press, 2020), pp. 24–25.

11. Levitsky and Ziblatt, *Tyranny of the Minority*, pp. 19–20.

12. Wood, *Empire of Liberty*, p. 284.

13. Wood, *Empire of Liberty*, p. 285.

14. Levitsky and Ziblatt, *Tyranny of the Minority*, pp. 19–20.

15. Foley, *Presidential Elections and Majority Rule*, pp. 27–28 (citing an August 23, 1823, letter from Madison to George Hay).

16. Josephson and Ross, "Repairing the Electoral College," p. 152; Robert M. Alexander, *Representation and the Electoral College* (Oxford University Press, 2019), pp. 49–51.

17. Josephson and Ross, "Repairing the Electoral College," pp. 152–153; Alexander, *Representation and the Electoral College*, pp. 50–51, 63.

18. Josephson and Ross, "Repairing the Electoral College," pp. 151–152; Alexander, *Representation and the Electoral College*, pp. 52–53.

19. Josephson and Ross, "Repairing the Electoral College," pp. 151–152.

20. James Madison seemed to favor direct election by a national popular vote as best in theory but rejected it because of the different suffrage rules in the free and slaveholding states. Alexander, *Representation and the Electoral College*, pp. 52–53. See also Alexander Keyssar, *Why Do We Still Have the Electoral College?* (Harvard University Press, 2020), p. 171.

21. Alexander, *Representation and the Electoral College*, p. 49.

22. Alexander, *Representation and the Electoral College*, p. 50.

23. Alexander, *Representation and the Electoral College*, p. 66 (Madison stated that "the president is to act for the people, not for States").

24. Alexander, *Representation and the Electoral College*, p. 53.

25. Alexander, *Representation and the Electoral College*, pp. 53–55.

26. Alexander, *Representation and the Electoral College*, pp. 127–129.

27. Alexander, *Representation and the Electoral College*, pp. 127–128.

28. *Chiafalo v. Washington*, 591 U.S. 578 (2020); *Ray v. Blair*, 343 U.S. 214 (1952).

29. Wood, *Empire of Liberty*, pp. 53, 157.

30. Wood, *Empire of Liberty*, p. 212.

31. Wood, *Empire of Liberty*, pp. 282–285.

32. Foley, *Presidential Elections and Majority Rule*, p. 24.

33. Foley, *Presidential Elections and Majority Rule*, p. 24.

34. Foley, *Presidential Elections and Majority Rule*, p. 24.

35. Alexander, *Representation and the Electoral College*, p. 54.

36. Schudson, *The Good Citizen*, pp. 87–88.

37. Schudson, *The Good Citizen*, pp. 50–51, 89.

38. Schudson, *The Good Citizen*, pp. 51–54.

39. Schudson, *The Good Citizen*, pp. 49–51.

40. Schudson, *The Good Citizen*, pp. 94, 101–103.

41. Schudson, *The Good Citizen*, pp. 94, 97–103.

42. Alexander, *Representation and the Electoral College*, p. 56 ("Preceding [the 1800] election, electors were pledging themselves to vote for a ticket").

43. Alexander, *Representation and the Electoral College*, pp. 56–57.

44. Josephson and Ross, "Repairing the Electoral College," p. 155. Additional changes they did make include reducing the number of top "finalists" who would advance to the House (or Senate, if no vice presidential candidate received a majority) in a contingent election.

45. Alexander, *Representation and the Electoral College*, pp. 124–127; Foley, *Presidential Elections and Majority Rule*, pp. 16–18.

46. Foley, *Presidential Elections and Majority Rule*, pp. 21–23.

47. Foley, *Presidential Elections and Majority Rule*, p. 68.

48. Alexander, *Representation and the Electoral College*, p. 5.

49. Keyssar, *Why Do We Still Have the Electoral College?*, pp. 36 (citing James Madison), 69.

50. Some states did initially adopt districting schemes, as anticipated by the framers. Delaware and Virginia used that method for the two presidential elections, as did Kentucky when it achieved statehood in time for the election of 1792 (the nation's second).

51. Keyssar, *Why Do We Still Have the Electoral College?*, p. 145; Alexander, *Representation and the Electoral College*, p. 5.

52. Foley, *Presidential Elections and Majority Rule*, p. 23.

53. Alexander, *Representation and the Electoral College*, p. 114. See also Foley, *Presidential Elections and Majority Rule*, p. 59; Josephson and Ross, "Repairing the Electoral College," p. 158.

54. Alexander, *Representation and the Electoral College*, p. 115.

55. Josephson and Ross, "Repairing the Electoral College," p. 158.

56. Josephson and Ross, "Repairing the Electoral College," p. 158.

57. Jackson was certainly right about the general effect of districting systems but was probably incorrect in his assessment that it cost him the election. In a head-to-head race, he would probably have lost the election of 1824 to John Quincy Adams. Foley, *Presidential Elections and Majority Rule*, pp. 51, 59–61.

58. Foley, *Presidential Elections and Majority Rule*, pp. 67–69.

59. The exceptions are Maine and Nebraska, both of which award two of their electoral votes to the winner of the statewide popular vote and the remainder to the winner of each of the state's congressional districts. Alexander, *Representation and the Electoral College*, pp. 37–38, 58; Keyssar, *Why Do We Still Have the Electoral College?*, pp. 142–143.

60. Foley, *Presidential Elections and Majority Rule*, pp. 69–72.

61. Foley, *Presidential Elections and Majority Rule*, pp. 69–72.

62. Foley, *Presidential Elections and Majority Rule*, pp. 69–72.

63. Foley, *Presidential Elections and Majority Rule*, pp. 78–81.

64. Foley, *Presidential Elections and Majority Rule*, pp. 78–81.

65. Eric Foner, *Reconstruction: America's Unfinished Revolution, 1863–1877* (Harper & Row, 1988), pp. 567–569.

66. Josephson and Ross, "Repairing the Electoral College," pp. 156–157.

67. Foner, *Reconstruction*, pp. 567–574, 577.

68. Foner, *Reconstruction*, pp. 575–577; Alexander, *Representation and the Electoral College*, pp. 15–16; Josephson and Ross, "Repairing the Electoral College," p. 185 (noting that during this time period Louisiana had two sitting governors and two canvassing boards, each claiming to speak for the state).

69. Foner, *Reconstruction*, pp. 581–582.

70. 3 U.S.C. §§ 5–7, 5–18 (1948); Cass R. Sunstein, "The Rule of Law v. 'Party Nature': Presidential Elections, the Constitution, the Electoral Count Act of 1887, the Horror of January 6, and the Electoral Count Reform Act of 2022," *Boston University Law Review* 103, no. 4 (October 2023): 1176.

71. Stephen A. Siegel, "The Conscientious Congressman's Guide to the Electoral Count Act of 1887," *Florida Law Review* 56, no. 3 (July 2004): 614.

72. Dan T. Coenen and Edward J. Larson, "Congressional Power over Presidential Elections: Lessons from the Past and Reforms for the Future," *William and Mary Law Review* 43, no. 3 (March 2002): 866–867.

73. Derek T. Muller, "Electoral Votes Regularly Given," *Georgia Law Review* 55, no. 4 (2021): 1532–1533.

74. Muller, "Electoral Votes Regularly Given"; Josephson and Ross, "Repairing the Electoral College," p. 182; Beverly J. Ross and William Josephson, "The Electoral College and the Popular Vote," *Journal of Law and Politics* 12, no. 4 (Fall 1996): 739.

75. Siegel, "The Conscientious Congressman's Guide to the Electoral Count Act of 1887," pp. 627–628.

76. See, for example, Muller, "Electoral Votes Regularly Given."

77. Muller, "Electoral Votes Regularly Given," p. 1539.

78. The January 6th Committee. *The January 6 Report: Findings from the Select Committee to Investigate the Attack on the U.S. Capitol with Reporting, Analysis and Visuals by The New York Times*, "The January 6 Report," (Twelve, 2022), pp. 262–268.

79. The January 6 Report, p. 268.

80. Jack Goldstein, "The Ministerial Role of the President of the Senate in Counting Electoral Votes: A Post-January 6 Perspective," *University of New Hampshire Law Review* 21, no. 2 (March 2023): 369.

81. The January 6 Report, pp. 18–20.

82. Electoral Count Reform Act of 2022, Pub. L. No. 117–328.

83. Derek T. Muller, "The Electoral Count Act: The Need for Reform" (testimony before the U.S. Senate Committee on Rules and Administration, August 3, 2022), pp. 8–9.

84. Muller, "The Electoral Count Act: The Need for Reform," p. 9.

85. Muller, "The Electoral Count Act: The Need for Reform," p. 10.

86. Electoral Count Reform Act of 2022, Pub. L. No. 117–328; see also Derek T. Muller, "Election Subversion and the Writ of Mandamus," *William and Mary Law Review* 65, no. 2 (November 2023): 327.

87. Muller, "The Electoral Count Act: The Need for Reform," pp. 10–11.

88. Muller, "The Electoral Count Act: The Need for Reform," pp. 10–11.

89. Muller, "The Electoral Count Act: The Need for Reform," pp. 14–15.

90. Muller, "The Electoral Count Act: The Need for Reform," p. 15.

91. Josephson and Ross, "Repairing the Electoral College," pp. 178–179.

92. Josephson and Ross, "Repairing the Electoral College," p. 178.

93. Joel K. Goldstein, "The Ministerial Role of the President of the Senate in Counting Electoral Votes: A Post-January 6 Perspective," *University of New Hampshire Law Review* 21, no. 2 (March 2023).

94. Muller, "The Electoral Count Act: The Need for Reform," pp. 15–16; Sunstein, "The Rule of Law v. 'Party Nature,'" p. 1177.

95. See generally Vasan Kesavan, "Is the Electoral Count Act Unconstitutional," *North Carolina Law Review* 80, no. 5 (June 2002): 1653 (raising concerns); Coenen and Larson, "Congressional Power over Presidential Elections," p. 851 (rebutting concerns); Siegel, "The Conscientious Congressman's Guide to the Electoral Count Act of 1887," p. 541 (examining the legislative history of the ECA).

96. Alexander, *Representation and the Electoral College*, p. 14.

97. Alexander, *Representation and the Electoral College*, p. 14.

98. Alexander, *Representation and the Electoral College*, pp. 18–19.

99. Alexander, *Representation and the Electoral College*, p. 16 (citing "Americans Have Long Questioned the Electoral College," Gallup News Service, November 16, 2000, http://news.gallup.com/poll/2305/americans-long-questioned-electoral-college.aspx).

100. Alexander, *Representation and the Electoral College*, p. 16 (citing "Americans Have Long Questioned the Electoral College").

101. "61% of Americans Support Abolishing Electoral College," Gallup News Service, September 24, 2020, https://news.gallup.com/poll/320744/americans-support-abolishing-electoral-college.aspx; "How Americans View Proposals to Change the Political System," Pew Research Center, September 19, 2023, https://www.pewresearch.org/politics/2023/09/19/how-americans-view-proposals-to-change-the-political-system/.

102. Article V. There also is an option through which a convention for proposing amendments can be called "on the application of the legislatures of two thirds of the several states."

103. U.S. Constitution, Article V.

104. The extent to which white southerners benefited in this era is striking. In the 1904 presidential election, for example, voters in Ohio cast roughly the same number of votes as the voters of nine southern states combined, but Ohio had only twenty-three electoral votes that year, while the southern states had ninety-nine. Keyssar, *Why Do We Still Have the Electoral College?*, p. 190.

105. Keyssar, *Why Do We Still Have the Electoral College?*, pp. 258–262.

106. Keyssar, *Why Do We Still Have the Electoral College?*, pp. 223–225.

107. Tara Ross, *Enlightened Democracy* (World Ahead, 2004), pp. 40–41, 83–84, 87–88, 158–160.

108. This often is articulated as an argument about "federalism." See Norman Williams, "Reforming the Electoral College: Federalism, Majoritarianism, and the Perils of Constitutional Change," *Georgetown Law Review* 100, no. 1 (March 2011): 4.

109. Keyssar, *Why Do We Still Have the Electoral College?*, p. 82.

110. Keyssar, *Why Do We Still Have the Electoral College?*, pp. 82, 197–198, 330.

111. "Facts and Myths," Delaware Corporate Law, accessed January 21, 2024, https://corplaw.delaware.gov/facts-and-myths/; "Alaska's Oil and Gas Industry," Alaska Resource Development Council, accessed January 21, 2024, https://www.akrdc.org/oil-and-gas; "Table H2: Urban and Rural," 2020 Decennial Census, accessed January 21, 2024, https://data.census.gov/table/DECENNIALDHC2020.H2?q=urban (showing 91% of Rhode Island's population living in an urban area); "Nation's Urban and Rural Populations Shift Following 2020 Census," U.S. Census Bureau, December 29, 2022, https://www.census.gov/newsroom/press-releases/2022/urban-rural-populations.html.

112. As discussed previously, Maine is one of two states (the other is Nebraska) that do not cast all of their electoral votes for the statewide winner. In 2024, Maine cast three of its votes for Harris and one for Trump.

113. "2020 Electoral College Results," U.S. National Archives and Records Administration, April 2021, https://www.archives.gov/electoral-college/2020.

114. "2024 Electoral College Results," U.S. National Archives and Records Administration, April 2021, https://www.archives.gov/electoral-college/2024.

115. Ross, *Enlightened Democracy*, pp. 87–88.

116. "Map of General-Election Campaign Events and TV Ad Spending by 2024 Presidential Candidates," National Popular Vote, accessed March 25, 2025, https://www.nationalpopularvote.com/almost-all-94-2024-presidential-campaign-was-concentrated-7-states.

117. "Map of General-Election Campaign Events and TV Ad Spending by 2024 Presidential Candidates," National Popular Vote.

118. "Map of General-Election Campaign Events and TV Ad Spending by 2024 Presidential Candidates," National Popular Vote.

119. U.S. States: Ranking by Population, World Population Review, https://worldpopulationreview.com/states.

120. See generally Mark Bohnhorst et al., "Presidential Election Reform: A Current National Imperative," *Lewis and Clark Law Review* 26, no. 2 (2022): 437, https://ssrn.com/abstract=3965096.

121. Bohnhorst et al., "Presidential Election Reform," pp. 444–445.

122. This argument is most commonly found in popular media outlets, such as the Cato Institute and Save our States. See, for example, John Samples, "Keep the Electoral College," Cato Institute, December 21, 2000, https://www.cato.org/commentary/keep-electoral-college#; and Sean Parnell, "National Popular Vote

Would Be Bad for Pennsylvania . . . and the Nation," Broad and Liberty, November 26, 2021, https://broadandliberty.com/2021/11/26/sean-parnell-national-popular-vote-would-be-bad-for-pennsylvania-and-the-nation/.

123. Alexander, *Representation and the Electoral College*, pp. 63–68.

124. Ricks, *First Principles*, pp. 198–199; Foley, *Presidential Elections and Majority Rule*, p. 15; Josephson and Ross, "Repairing the Electoral College," p. 153 (noting that framers expected the electors to vote for at least one man of a "continental reputation").

125. Ricks, *First Principles*, pp. 226–227 (citing Madison's writing from October 1791 that "in all political societies, different interests and parties arise out of the nature of things, and the great art of politicians lies in making them checks and balances to each other").

126. Foley, *Presidential Elections and Majority Rule*, pp. 13–15.

127. See for example Keith E. Whittington, "Originalism, Constitutional Construction, and the Problem of Faithless Electors," *Arizona Law Review* 59, no. 4 (2017): 903.

128. See, for example, Tara Ross, *Enlightened Democracy*, p. 114.

129. Foley, *Presidential Elections and Majority Rule*, p. 15.

130. Foley, *Presidential Elections and Majority Rule*, p. 15.

131. Keyssar, *Why Do We Still Have the Electoral College?*, pp. 9–10, 361; Alexander, *Representation and the Electoral College*, pp. 86–90. See also "Exploring the 2024 Presidential Battleground States," accessed August 2, 2025, https://prri.org/spotlight/exploring-the-2024-presidential-battleground-states-inside-the-issues/.

132. Keyssar, *Why Do We Still Have the Electoral College?*, pp. 66–68.

133. Keyssar, *Why Do We Still Have the Electoral College?*, pp. 80–81.

134. Keyssar, *Why Do We Still Have the Electoral College?*, p. 342.

135. Keyssar, *Why Do We Still Have the Electoral College?*, p. 343.

136. Keyssar, *Why Do We Still Have the Electoral College?*, p. 9. For Wisconsin district maps, see "Wisconsin State Senate," Ballotpedia, accessed January 19, 2024, https://ballotpedia.org/Wisconsin_State_Senate; "Wisconsin State Assembly," Ballotpedia, accessed January 19, 2024, https://ballotpedia.org/Wisconsin_State_Assembly; "United States Congressional Delegations from Wisconsin," Ballotpedia, accessed January 19, 2024, https://ballotpedia.org/United_States_congressional_delegations_from_Wisconsin. For North Carolina district maps, see "North Carolina State Senate," Ballotpedia, accessed January 19, 2024, https://ballotpedia.org/North_Carolina_State_Senate; "North Carolina House of Representatives," Ballotpedia, accessed January 19, 2024, https://

ballotpedia.org/North_Carolina_House_of_Representatives; "United States Congressional Delegations from North Carolina," Ballotpedia, accessed January 19, 2024, https://ballotpedia.org/United_States_congressional_delegations_from_North_Carolina.

137. Maurice Duverger, *Political Parties: Their Organization and Activity in the Modern State*, trans. Barbara and Robert North, 3rd ed. (Harper & Row, 1964); Alexander, *Representation and the Electoral College*, p. 9.

138. Josephson and Ross, "Repairing the Electoral College," p. 158; Fuentes-Rohwer and Charles, "The Electoral College, the Right to Vote, and Our Federalism: A Comment on a Lasting Institution," p. 905 ("Without the unit rule, a third party or third-party candidate or reasonable political strength would almost always prevent either of the two major parties from getting an Electoral College majority"); see also Keyssar, *Why Do We Still Have the Electoral College?*, pp. 98–100.

139. Foley, *Presidential Elections and Majority Rule*, pp. 126–131.

140. Keyssar, *Why Do We Still Have the Electoral College?*, p. 90.

141. Richard H. Pildes and G. Michael Parsons, "The Legality of Ranked-Choice Voting," *California Law Review* 109 (October 2021): 1773, https://ssrn.com/abstract=3563257.

142. For an interesting discussion of how ranked-choice voting could intersect with the National Popular Vote Compact, see Rob Richie et al., "Toward a More Perfect Union: Integrating Ranked Choice Voting with the National Popular Vote Compact," *Harvard Law and Policy Review* 15, no. 1 (Winter 2020): 145.

143. Pildes and Parsons, "The Legality of Ranked-Choice Voting," pp. 1775–1776.

144. Pildes and Parsons, "The Legality of Ranked-Choice Voting," pp. 1782, 1787.

145. Pildes and Parsons, "The Legality of Ranked-Choice Voting," pp. 1775–1776.

146. Graham Paul Goldberg, "Georgia's Runoff Election Has Run Its Course," *Georgia Law Review* 54, no. 3 (2020): 1063.

147. Josephson and Ross, "Repairing the Electoral College," pp. 149–150.

148. Whittington, "Originalism, Constitutional Construction, and the Problem of Faithless Electors," p. 914 (citing Hamilton).

149. Keyssar, *Why Do We Still Have the Electoral College?*, pp. 5–6 (districting); Alexander, *Representation and the Electoral College*, pp. 129–130 (discussing the "Hamiltonian electors" debate after the 2016 election).

150. Keyssar, *Why Do We Still Have the Electoral College?*, p. 7.

151. Wilfred U. Codrington III, "So Goes the Nation: The Constitution, the Compact, What the American West Can Tell Us About How We'll Choose the President in 2020 and Beyond," *Columbia Law Review* 120, no. 2 (March 2020): 43, https://ssrn.com/abstract=3619144.

152. Codrington, "So Goes the Nation," p. 45.

153. National Popular Vote, accessed January 13, 2024, https://www.national popularvote.com/.

154. William Josephson, "States May Statutorily Bind Presidential Electors, the Myth of the National Popular Vote, the Reality of Elector Unit Rule Voting and Old Light on Three-Fifths of Other Persons," *University of Miami Law Review* 76, no. 3 (June 2022): 761.

155. U.S. Constitution, Article I, Section 10, Clause 1.

156. U.S. Constitution, Article I, Section 10, Clause 3.

157. Note that our usage of "treaties" to refer to agreements with foreign nations does not appear to have been a distinguishing factor in the founding era. Derek T. Muller, "The Compact Clause and the National Popular Vote Interstate Compact," *Election Law Journal* 6, no. 4 (2007): 372; Jennifer S. Hendricks, "Popular Election of the President: Using or Abusing the Electoral College?" *Election Law Journal* 7, no. 3 (2008): 218.

158. For arguments for and against the constitutionality of the compact under these clauses, see Muller, "National Popular Vote Interstate Compact," p. 382; Akhil Reed Amar and Vikram David Amar, "How to Achieve Direct National Election of the President Without Amending the Constitution," *FindLaw*, December 28, 2001, https://supreme.findlaw.com/legal-commentary/how-to -achieve-direct-national-election-of-the-president-without-amending-the -constitution.html; and Hendricks, "Popular Election of the President," p. 218.

159. For an in-depth examination of how this might play out, see Edward A. Hartnett, "The Pathological Perspective and Presidential Elections," *SMU Law Review* 73, no. 3 (January 2020): 445, 470.

160. Norman R. Williams, "Why the National Popular Vote Compact Is Unconstitutional," *BYU Law Review* 2012, no. 5 (December 2012): 1523.

161. See generally Derek T. Muller, "The Electoral College and the Federal Popular Vote," *Harvard Law and Policy Review* 15, no. 1 (Winter 2020): 129.

Chapter 4

1. *Republican National Committee v. Democratic National Committee*, 589 U.S. 423, 432, 140 S. Ct. 1205, 1211 (2020) (Justice Ginsburg, dissenting).

2. U.S. Election Assistance Commission, Report to the 117th Congress, Election Administration and Voting Survey 2020 Comprehensive Report, p. 61 (discussing state registration procedures); pp. 69–72 (discussing state vote-by-mail procedures).

3. Alexander Keyssar, *The Right to Vote: The Contested History of Democracy in the United States*, rev. ed. (Basic Books, 2009), p. 4.

4. Michael J. Klarman, *The Framers' Coup: The Making of the United States Constitution* (Oxford University Press, 2016), pp. 178–180.

5. Keyssar, *The Right to Vote*, p. 4; Klarman, *The Framers' Coup*, pp. 178–180.

6. See generally Ralph Ketcham, ed., *The Anti-Federalist Papers and the Constitutional Convention Debates* (Signet Classics, 2003), pp. 135–137 (citing the Philadelphia Convention Debates); Klarman, *The Framers' Coup*, pp. 178–181.

7. See generally Ketcham, *The Anti-Federalist Papers*, pp. 142–148.

8. Klarman, *The Framers' Coup*, pp. 178–181.

9. Klarman, *The Framers' Coup*, pp. 178–181.

10. See generally Ketcham, *The Anti-Federalist Papers*, p. 136.

11. Klarman, *The Framers' Coup*, pp. 241–243; Pauline Maier, *Ratification: The People Debate the Constitution, 1787–1788* (Simon & Schuster, 2010), pp. 139–140.

12. Under the 1787 Constitution, U.S. senators were chosen by members of the state legislature rather than by voters, which is why this provision only addresses elections for the House of Representatives. Identical language was included in the Seventeenth Amendment (ratified in 1912), which established direct election of senators by the people of each state.

13. Klarman, *The Framers' Coup*, p. 342.

14. The final clause of this provision prohibited the federal government from requiring that the state legislature, who under the original Constitution choose the state's U.S. senators, meet to do so at inconvenient places different from its usual meeting places. This was a maneuver King George used to disempower colonial assemblies prior to the Revolutionary War, so it was clearly on the founders' mind as a thing to avoid.

15. *Harper v. Virginia State Board of Elections*, 383 U.S. 663 (1966).

16. Dean Franita Tolson has argued that the Qualifications Clause imposes more voter-friendly duties on states than first appears. See, for example, Franita

Tolson, "Protecting Political Participation Through the Voter Qualifications Clause of Article I," *Boston College Law Review* 56, no. 1 (January 2014): 191.

17. Pauline Maier, *Ratification*, p. 119 (Pennsylvania), 172–173 (Massachusetts), 174 (Bishop proposal in Massachusetts), 307 (Virginia), and 362 (New York).

18. See generally Ketcham, *The Anti-Federalist Papers*, pp. 217–218.

19. See generally Ketcham, *The Anti Federalist Papers*, pp. 342–343.

20. Maier, *Ratification*, p. 173.

21. Maier, *Ratification*, p. 114 (citing Merrill Jensen et al., eds., *The Documentary History of the Ratification of the Constitution: Volume II* (Wisconsin Historical Society Press, 2021), pp. 557–558, 563–566, 577–578.).

22. Maier, *Ratification*, p. 173.

23. Federalist 59.

24. Federalist 59.

25. *Ex parte Siebold*, 100 U.S. 371 (1879).

26. 570 U.S. 1 (2013).

27. *Arizona v. Inter Tribal Council of Arizona, Inc.*, 570 U.S. 1, 5 (2013).

28. *Inter Tribal*, 5–6.

29. *Inter Tribal*, 4–5, 6.

30. *Inter Tribal*, 4–5.

31. *Inter Tribal*, 6.

32. *Inter Tribal*, 6.

33. U.S. Constitution, Article VI, Clause 2.

34. *Inter Tribal*, 8–9.

35. *Inter Tribal*, 14.

36. *Inter Tribal*, 17.

37. *Inter Tribal*, 17–18.

38. *Inter Tribal*, 17–18.

39. *Inter Tribal*, 17.

40. *Kobach v. United States Election Assistance Commission*, 772 F.3d 1183, 1196–1197 (United States Court of Appeals for the Tenth Circuit, 2014).

41. *Mi Famila Vota v. Fontes*, No. 24–3188 District of Arizona, August 1, 2024).

42. *Mi Famila Vota.*

43. Brenda Write, "Young v. Fordice: Challenging Duel Registration Under Section 5 of the Voting Rights Act," *Mississippi College Law Review*, no. 18 (1998).

44. *Mi Famila Vota.*

45. U.S. Constitution, Article II, Section 1. The Electors Clause does not

have the equivalent of a times, places, and manners provision. This has led to a disagreement about the extent to which federal election laws can govern presidential (rather than just congressional) elections. Michael Morley, "Dismantling the Unitary Electoral System? Uncooperative Federalism in State and Local Elections," *Northwestern University Law Review Online* 111 (February 2017): 105–108; *Mi Famila Vota*, p. 993.

46. Trip Gabriel and Stephanie Saul, "Could State Legislatures Pick Electors to Vote for Trump? Not Likely," *New York Times*, January 5, 2021, https://www.nytimes.com/article/electors-vote.html.

47. 531 U.S. 98 (2000).

48. *Bush v. Gore*, 531 U.S. 98, 115 (2000).

49. *Texas v. Pennsylvania*, 141 S.Ct. 1230 (2020) (petition and denial of motion by the State of Texas for leave to file a complaint).

50. Gabriel and Saul, "Could State Legislatures Pick Electors to Vote for Trump? Not Likely."

51. Alan Feuer and Zach Montague, "Over 30 Trump Campaign Lawsuits Have Failed. Some Rulings Are Scathing," *New York Times*, December 10, 2020, https://www.nytimes.com/2020/11/25/us/elections/trump-campaign-lawsuits.html.

52. 576 U.S. 787 (2015).

53. 143 S. Ct. 2065 (2023).

54. *Rucho v. Common Cause*, 588 U.S. 684 (2019).

55. *Baker v. Carr*, 369 U.S. 186, 198, 211 (1962).

56. *Tafflin v. Levitt*, 493 U.S. 455 (1990) ("Under our federal system, the States possess sovereignty concurrent with that of the Federal Government, subject only to limitations imposed by the Supremacy Clause. Under this system of dual sovereignty, we have consistently held that state courts have inherent authority, and are thus presumptively competent, to adjudicate claims arising under the laws of the United States"). See also Federalist 82 (Hamilton explaining that, despite the grant of jurisdiction to federal courts, state courts retain their previous authority unless exclusive delegation of jurisdiction exists).

57. *Arizona State Legislature v. Arizona Independent Redistricting Commission*, 576 U.S. 787, 791–792 (2015).

58. *Arizona Independent Redistricting Commission*, 793–795.

59. *Arizona Independent Redistricting Commission*, 795.

60. The understanding of state legislatures as creatures of the state is very old. See Klarman, *The Framers' Coup*, p. 415 (citing James Madison).

61. *Arizona Independent Redistricting Commission*, 813.

62. *Arizona Independent Redistricting Commission*, 808.

63. *Arizona Independent Redistricting Commission*, 809.

64. *Arizona Independent Redistricting Commission*, 816–817.

65. *Arizona Independent Redistricting Commission*, 814–816.

66. *Arizona Independent Redistricting Commission*, 815–816, 817–818, 820.

67. *Arizona Independent Redistricting Commission*, 814–816.

68. *Arizona Independent Redistricting Commission*, 816.

69. *Arizona Independent Redistricting Commission*, 816–818.

70. *Arizona Independent Redistricting Commission*, 816–818.

71. *Arizona Independent Redistricting Commission*, 827–829 (Chief Justice Roberts, dissenting).

72. *Arizona Independent Redistricting Commission*, 828 (Chief Justice Roberts, dissenting).

73. *Arizona Independent Redistricting Commission*, 832–833 (Chief Justice Roberts, dissenting).

74. *Arizona Independent Redistricting Commission*, 841–842 (Chief Justice Roberts, dissenting).

75. *Arizona Independent Redistricting Commission*, 848–849 (Chief Justice Roberts, dissenting).

76. 600 U.S. 1 (2023).

77. Carolyn Shapiro, "The Independent State Legislature Theory, Federal Courts, and State Law," *University of Chicago Law Review* 90, no. 1 (2023): 137, 140–141.

78. *Harper v. Hall*, 380 N.C. 317 (Supreme Court of North Carolina, 2022).

79. Michael Wines, "North Carolina Court Says G.O.P. Political Maps Violate State Constitution," *New York Times*, February 4, 2022, https://www.nytimes.com/2022/02/04/us/north-carolina-redistricting-gerrymander-unconstitutional.html.

80. *Moore v. Harper*, 600 U.S. 1, 2–3 (2023).

81. *Harper v. Hall*, 380 N.C. 317 (Supreme Court of North Carolina, 2022). After an intervening judicial election, the state supreme court changed its mind and held that gerrymandering did not violate the state constitution. That switch was purely a matter of state law.

82. *Moore v. Harper*, 14–15.

83. Shapiro, "The Independent State Legislature Theory, Federal Courts, and State Law," p. 137 (describing Independent State Legislature Theory as "as-

sert[ing] that state constitutions' substantive provisions cannot apply to state election laws governing federal elections.").

84. *Moore*, 17–18.

85. See, for example, *Moore*, 11–19.

86. *Moore*, 15.

87. *Moore*, 29.

88. *Moore*, 28–29.

89. Election Assistance Commission, "Report to the 117th Congress, Election Administration and Voting Survey 2020 Comprehensive Report" (2020), pp. 2, 62–63 (identifying states offering online or same-day registration).

90. Election Assistance Commission, "Report," p. 54.

91. Election Assistance Commission, "Report," pp. 76–77.

92. "State Primary Election Types," National Conference of State Legislatures, June 22, 2023, https://www.ncsl.org/elections-and-campaigns/state -primary-election-types.

93. Pub.L. 103–31, 52 U.S.C. §§ 20501–20511 (1993); see also Election Assistance Commission, "Report," p. 115.

94. 52 U.S.C. § 20507(a)(1)(B); Election Assistance Commission, "Report," p. 116.

95. 52 U.S.C. § 21083(b).

96. 52 U.S.C. § 21083(b).

97. 52 U.S.C. § 21083(b)(3) (stating that the other provisions of the statute are inapplicable to persons who already registered to vote and already submitted acceptable identification at the time of registration). HAVA has not been amended to explicitly cover online registration, which many states have implemented. See "The Help America Vote Act of 2002: Overview and Ongoing Role in Election Administration Policy," Congressional Research Service, May 8, 2023, https://crsreports.congress.gov/product/pdf/R/R46949; Election Assistance Commission, "Report," p. 61. It seems likely that HAVA requirements apply already, because online registration mirrors more traditional ways of registering to vote. See Election Assistance Commission, "Report," p. 61.

98. 52 U.S.C. § 21083(a)(5)(B); see also Election Assistance Commission, "Report," pp. 56–58; "Election Security Rumor vs. Reality," Department of Homeland Security, Cybersecurity and Infrastructure Security Agency, accessed August 29, 2023, https://www.cisa.gov/topics/election-security (discussing database cross-checks mandated by HAVA). For the relationship between HAVA and NVRA, see Election Assistance Commission, "Report," pp. 117.

99. Election Assistance Commission, "Report," pp. 119, 135–137.

100. Election Assistance Commission, "Report," p. 59 (describing lag in states using different processes).

101. Election Assistance Commission, "Report," pp. 11–12, 69–72.

102. Election Assistance Commission, "Report," p. 11. See also "A Brief History of Vote By Mail in Oregon," Multnomah County Elections Division, accessed October 1, 2023, https://www.multco.us/elections/brief-history-vote-mail-oregon; Utah House Bill 172 (2012), https://le.utah.gov/~2012/bills/static/HB0172.html.

103. Election Assistance Commission, "Report," p. 11.

104. Election Assistance Commission, "Report," p. 11.

105. The U.S. Election Assistance Commission publishes elaborate chain-of-custody "best practices" to assist states in designing systems to track this information. "Best Practices: Chain of Custody v.11," U.S. Election Assistance Commission, July 13, 2021, https://www.eac.gov/sites/default/files/bestpractices/Chain_of_Custody_Best_Practices.pdf.

106. Election Assistance Commission, "Best Practices: Chain of Custody v.11."

107. HAVA requires all states to provide a unique identifier for every registered voter. 52 U.S.C. § 21083(a)(1)(A)(iii); "State Voter Registration Databases: Immediate Actions and Future Improvements, Interim Report," National Research Council (2008), https://nap.nationalacademies.org/catalog/12173/state-voter-registration-databases-immediate-actions-and-future-improvements-interim.

108. "Voting Outside the Polling Places: Absentee, All-Mail and Other Voting at Home Options, Table 8: How States Verify Absentee Ballot Applications," National Conference of State Legislatures, July 12, 2022, https://www.ncsl.org/elections-and-campaigns/table-8-how-states-verify-absentee-ballot-applications. See also "Voting Outside the Polling Places: Absentee, All-Mail and Other Voting at Home Options, Table 14: How States Verify Voted Absentee/Mail Ballots," National Conference of State Legislatures, March 15, 2022, https://www.ncsl.org/elections-and-campaigns/table-14-how-states-verify-voted-absentee-mail-ballots.

109. "State Voter Registration Databases: Immediate Actions and Future Improvements, Interim Report," National Research Council (2008), https://nap.nationalacademies.org/catalog/12173/state-voter-registration-databases-immediate-actions-and-future-improvements-interim.

110. Double registration is not uncommon, for the reasons discussed earlier. In the rare event that actual "double voting" does occur, it is almost always in two different districts and often involves individuals who own property in both jurisdictions and believe they can vote in both. "Double Voting," National Conference of State Legislatures, October 25, 2022, https://www.ncsl.org/elections-and-campaigns/double-voting.

111. Election Assistance Commission, "Report," p. 64.

112. Election Assistance Commission, "Report," pp. 26, 76–77.

113. U.S. Election Assistance Commission, "Electronic Poll Book Report," June 2023, https://www.eac.gov/sites/default/files/2023-07/Electronic_Poll_Book_Report_Final_508.pdf.

114. See "Election Security Rumor vs. Reality" ("Upon receipt of a mail-in/absentee ballot request form, election officials implement varying procedures to verify the identity and eligibility of the applicant prior to sending the applicant a mail-in/absentee ballot. Such procedures include checking the signature and information submitted on the form against the corresponding voter registration record, as well as ensuring that multiple mail-in/absentee ballots are not sent in response to applications using the same voter's information"). "Voting Outside the Polling Places: Absentee, All-Mail and Other Voting at Home Options, Table 8: How States Verify Absentee Ballot Applications," National Conference of State Legislatures, July 12, 2022, https://www.ncsl.org/elections-and-campaigns/table-8-how-states-verify-absentee-ballot-applications.

115. "Best Practices: Chain of Custody v.11," U.S. Election Assistance Commission, July 13, 2021, https://www.eac.gov/sites/default/files/bestpractices/Chain_of_Custody_Best_Practices.pdf. Each of the "disputed" 2020 states followed these procedures. See "Voting Equipment," Arizona Secretary of State, accessed September 29, 2023, https://azsos.gov/elections/about-elections/voting-equipment; "Subject 183-1-12, Preparation for and Conduct of Primaries and Elections, Rules and Regulations of the State of Georgia," accessed September 29, 2023, https://rules.sos.state.ga.us/gac/183-1-12; "Election Security in Michigan," Michigan Bureau of Elections, accessed September 29, 2023, https://www.michigan.gov/-/media/Project/Websites/sos/21lawensn/Security_best_practices.pdf?rev=883bafc1f98b45a69f67cb21ab05b2bc; "Nevada Voting System Testing and Security Diagram: Chain of Custody," Nevada Secretary of State, accessed September 29, 2023, https://www.nvsos.gov/sos/home/showpublisheddocument/4498/636584327657330000; "Election Security in Pennsylvania," Pennsylvania Department of State, accessed September 29, 2023, https://www.vote.pa.gov/

About-Elections/Pages/Election-Security.aspx; and "Wisconsin's Commitment to Election Integrity," Wisconsin Election Commission, accessed September 29, 2023, https://elections.wi.gov/wisconsins-commitment-election-integrity.

116. Election Assistance Commission, "Report," p. 79 (regarding testing procedures); and Election Assistance Commission, "EAC Testing & Certification Program," (2021), p. 7, https://www.eac.gov/voting-equipment/testing-and-certi fication-program (regarding internet disabled).

117. Election Assistance Commission, "Report," p. 25 (reporting that in 2020 only nine states failed to provide a paper audit trail in one or more of their voting jurisdictions: Arkansas, Indiana, Kansas, Kentucky, Louisiana, Mississippi, New Jersey, Tennessee, and Texas).

118. Election Assistance Commission, "EAC Testing & Certification Program," p. 8 (auditability of voting systems requires paper-based verifiable systems).

119. "Election Administration at State and Local Levels," National Conference of State Legislatures, accessed August 29, 2023, p. 7, https://www.ncsl.org/ elections-and-campaigns/election-administration-at-state-and-local-levels.

120. Voting jurisdictions in the United States vary significantly, with some units containing only a few hundred voters while the largest has more than 4.7 million voters. "Report: DHS Has Secured the Nation's Election Systems, but Work Remains to Protect the Infrastructure," Office of the Inspector General, Department of Homeland Security, October 22, 2020, p. 3, https://www.oig.dhs .gov/sites/default/files/assets/2020-10/OIG-21-01-Oct20.pdf.

121. "EAVS Deep Dive: Poll Workers and Polling Places," Election Assistance Commission, 2017, https://www.eac.gov/sites/default/files/document_li brary/files/EAVSDeepDive_pollworkers_pollingplacess_nov17.pdf; see also Wisconsin Statute § 7.52(1)(a).

122. Election Assistance Commission, "Report," p. 4.

123. Election Assistance Commission, Quick Start Guide: Canvassing & Certifying an Election, https://www.eac.gov/sites/default/files/electionofficials/ QuickStartGuides/Canvass_and_Certification_EAC_Quick_Start_Guide_508 .pdf.

124. Election Assistance Commission, "Report," pp. 81–84, 108–113 (describing recount, audit, and certification procedures); National Conference of State Legislatures, *Election Administration at State and Local Levels*, November 1, 2022 (identifying the chief elections officer of each state).

125. Michael Beckel, Amelia Minkin, Amisa Ratliff, Ariana Rojas, Kathryn

Thomas, and Adrien Van Voorhis, "Report: The High Cost of High Turnover," Issue One, September 26, 2023, https://issueone.org/articles/the-high-cost-of -high-turnover/ (detailing the effects of harassment after 2020 on election official retention). See also "Secretary of State's Office Opens Investigation into Coffee County's Handling of Recount," Georgia Secretary of State, December 9, 2020, https://sos.ga.gov/news/secretary-states-office-opens-investigation-coffee -countys-handling-recount; "State Board Removes 2 Surry County Board of Elections Members," North Carolina State Board of Elections, March 28, 2023, https://www.ncsbe.gov/news/press-releases/2023/03/28/state-board-removes-2 -surry-county-board-elections-members; Summer Hom, "Cochise County Cer- tifies Election," Arizona Public Media, December 1, 2022, https://news.azpm. org/p/news-splash/2022/12/1/213965-cochise-county-certifies-election/. See, for example, Doug Bock Clark, "Some Election Officials Refused to Certify Results. Few Were Held Accountable," March 9, 2023, https://www.propublica.org/arti cle/election-officials-refused-certify-results-few-held-accountable.

126. "Contested Elections," updated November 5, 2024, https://www.ncsl.org /elections-and-campaigns/contested-election-deadlines.

127. Lauren Miller and Will Wilder, "Certification and Non-Discretion: A Guide to Protecting the 2014 Elections," *Stanford Law and Policy Review* (2024).

128. Election Assistance Commission, "Report," p. ii.

129. See "Joint Statement of Elections Infrastructure Government Coordi- nating Council and the Election Infrastructure Sector Coordinating Executive Committees," Department of Homeland Security, Cybersecurity and Infra- structure Security Agency, November 12, 2020, https://www.cisa.gov/news -events/news/joint-statement-elections-infrastructure-government-coordinating -council-election ("The November 3rd election was the most secure in American History. . . . There is no evidence that any voting system deleted or lost votes, changed votes, or was in any way compromised").

130. *Judicial Watch, Inc. v. Boockvar*, 524 F. Supp. 3d 399 (U.S. District Court, Middle District of Pennsylvania, Harrisburg Division) (2021).

131. Craig Gilbert and Patrick Marley, "Biden Declared Winner in Wiscon- sin with 20,000 Vote Margin; Trump Campaign Vows Request for Recount," *Milwaukee Journal Sentinel*, November 4, 2020, https://www.jsonline.com/story/ news/politics/elections/2020/11/04/wisconsin-results-down-wire-again -milwaukee-ballot-count/6123344002/.

132. See, for example, "Report: DHS Has Secured the Nation's Election Sys-

tems, but Work Remains to Protect the Infrastructure," Office of the Inspector General, Department of Homeland Security, October 22, 2020, pp. 14–28, https://www.oig.dhs.gov/sites/default/files/assets/2020-10/OIG-21-01-Oct20.pdf.

133. ERIC was the most comprehensive effort to do this but came under attack after it was featured in a sprawling conspiracy theory spread online after the 2020 election. See Jesse Wegman, "Republicans Are No Longer Calling This Election Program a 'Godsend,'" *New York Times* (June 6, 2023), https://www.ny times.com/2023/06/06/opinion/republican-voter-fraud-eric.html.

134. See Grace Gordon, Michael Thorning, and Matthew Weil, "Reimagining Federal Election Funding," Bipartisan Policy Center, 2022, https://bipartisan policy.org/report/reimagining-federal-election-funding; Joseph Marks and Aaron Schaffer, "Election Officials Want More Funds to Combat Midterm Election Cyber Threats," *Washington Post*, February 17, 2022, https://www.washing tonpost.com/politics/2022/02/17/election-officials-want-more-funds-combat-mid term-election-cyber-threats.

135. Richard H. Pildes, "Election Law in an Age of Distrust," *Stanford Law Review Online* 74 (May 2022): 100, https://www.stanfordlawreview.org/online/ election-law-in-an-age-of-distrust/.

136. See, for example, "The Canvass: June 2022," National Conference of State Legislatures, June 1, 2022, https://www.ncsl.org/newsletter/details/the-can vass-june-2022 (detailing electoral reform enactments reflecting these recommendations).

137. In the aftermath of the 2020 election, election officials in at least three states allegedly allowed activists aligned with Donald Trump to gain unauthorized access to voting machines. Election administrators in Michigan and in Coffee County, Georgia have faced charges; charges have not been filed in relation to an alleged incident in Mesa County, Colorado. See "Indictment," *The State of Georgia v. Donald John Trump*, 2023SC188947 (Fulton County Superior Court, 2023), https://www.fultonclerk.org/DocumentCenter/View/2108/CRIM INAL-INDICTMENT (naming as defendants two individuals in Coffee County, Georgia); "Michigan Attorney General Dana Nessel Charges 16 'False Electors' with Election Law and Forgery Felonies," Michigan Department of Attorney General, July 18, 2023, https://www.michigan.gov/ag/news/press -releases/2023/07/18/michigan-attorney-general-dana-nessel-charges-16-false -electors; "Mesa County Grand Jury Indictment," *People of the State of Colorado v. Tina Peters*, 21CR100, March 8, 2022, https://ewscripps.brightspotcdn.com/de/ 66/cbbec78e4275942b9fecfd516405/indictment.pdf. Other jurisdictions, such as

Maricopa County, Arizona, authorized private entities to review their data and equipment after the 2020 election. See "BPC Elections and Election Officials: Cyber Ninjas' Report Shows Glaring Ignorance of Election Administration," Bipartisan Policy Center, September 24, 2021, https://bipartisanpolicy.org/press -release/bpc-elections-and-election-officials-cyber-ninjas-report-shows-glaring -ignorance-of-election-administration/

138. Hand-counting legislation has been introduced in New Hampshire, Arizona, Colorado, Missouri, Washington, and West Virginia. See Holly Ramer and Christina A. Cassidy, "Some in GOP Want Ballots to Be Counted by Hand, Not Machines," AP News, March 12, 2022, https://apnews.com/article/2022 -midterm-elections-new-hampshire-nevada-donald-trump-elections-3f6785364 fd52655cbd034f0708c6f0f.

139. Arizona Senate Bill 1135 (2023).

140. Stephen Ansolabehere, Barry C. Burden, Kenneth R. Mayer, and Charles Stewart III, "Learning from Recounts," *Election Law Journal* 17, no. 2 (2018): 100.

Chapter 5

1. Fannie Lou Hamer, speech at the 1964 Democratic National Convention, August 22, 1964. Mississippi Department of Archives and History. https://www .mdah.ms.gov/new/wp-content/uploads/2014/08/Lesson-Five-Mississippi-in -1964-A-Turning-Point.pdf.

2. For a discussion of how the values of the Reconstruction Constitution intersect with that of the 1787 Constitution, see Kermit Roosevelt, *The Nation That Never Was: Reconstructing America's Story* (University of Chicago Press, 2022).

3. Eric Foner, *Reconstruction: America's Unfinished Revolution, 1863–1877* (HarperCollins, 1988), p. 354.

4. Foner, *Reconstruction*, pp. 354–355.

5. Manisha Sinha, *The Rise and Fall of the Second American Republic: Reconstruction 1860–1920* (Liveright, 2024), pp. 266–279.

6. Sinha, *The Rise and Fall of the Second American Republic*, pp. 270–279.

7. See generally *Tennessee v. Lane*, 541 U.S. 509, 520 (2004) ("When Congress seeks to remedy or prevent unconstitutional discrimination § 5 authorizes it to enact prophylactic legislation proscribing practices that are discriminatory in effect, if not in intent, to carry out the basic objectives of the Equal Protection Clause"); *Nevada Department of Human Resources v. Hibbs*, 538 U.S. 721, 727–728 (2003).

8. Travis Crum, "The Lawfulness of the Fifteenth Amendment," *Notre Dame Law Review* 97, no. 4 (April 2022): 1553–1556.

9. Many Americans credit the Emancipation Proclamation, signed by Abraham Lincoln on January 1, 1863, with ending slavery in the United States. But the Proclamation was not nearly that comprehensive. Signed by Lincoln while the nation was still embroiled in civil war, it applied only to enslaved people held in areas that had seceded from the Union. It did not cover the slaveholding border states that had not joined the Confederacy (Delaware, Maryland, Kentucky, Missouri, and West Virginia). The Proclamation also rested on shaky legal grounds. Lincoln had not issued it in accordance with any law enacted by Congress but rather as a "war powers" measure. That meant that its authority both relied on and was limited to whatever authority a president has to act in the absence of congressional authority as the commander in chief of the armed forces. The extent of that authority is underspecified in the Constitution and was (and remains) hotly contested. So while the Emancipation Proclamation is rightly celebrated as a milestone for freedom in America, by its own terms it only purported to liberate around 3 million of the approximately 3.8 million enslaved people living in the United States. See generally Foner, *Reconstruction*, pp. 1–5.

10. Eric Foner, *The Second Founding: How the Civil War and Reconstruction Remade the Constitution* (Norton, 2019), pp. 11–13.

11. Aziz Rana, *The Two Faces of American Freedom* (Harvard University Press, 2010), pp. 50–55.

12. Rana, *The Two Faces of American Freedom*, pp. 50–55; Foner, *The Second Founding*, pp. 6–17.

13. Foner, *The Second Founding*, pp. 6, 42; Kurt Lash, "Enforcing the Rights of Due Process: The Original Relationship Between the Fourteenth Amendment and the 1866 Civil Rights Act," *Georgetown Law Journal* 106, no. 5 (2018): 1402.

14. Foner, *The Second Founding*, p. 7.

15. Alexander Tsesis, "Interpreting the Thirteenth Amendment," *University of Pennsylvania Journal of Constitutional Law* 11, no. 5 (July 2009): 1338–1340.

16. Foner, *The Second Founding*, pp. 7, 40–41.

17. Civil Rights Act of 1866, 14 Stat. 27 (April 9, 1866).

18. Civil Rights Act of 1866, section 1.

19. For a general discussion of this issue, see Van Gosse, *The First Reconstruction: Black Politics in America from the Revolution to the Civil War* (University of North Carolina Press, 2021), pp. 2, 5–6. As Gosse documents, questions of polit-

ical rights and citizenship for Black men had always been contested. Reconstruction, he argues, was a continuation of this longstanding battle.

20. Foner, *The Second Founding*, pp. 61.

21. Foner, *The Second Founding*, pp. 59–60.

22. Foner, *The Second Founding*, pp. 59–60.

23. Foner, *The Second Founding*, pp. 58–62.

24. Foner, *The Second Founding*, p. 90.

25. *Barron v. Baltimore*, 32 U.S. 243 (1833).

26. Foner, *The Second Founding*, pp. 61–62.

27. Michael Kent Curtis, "The Fourteenth Amendment: Recalling What the Court Forgot," *Drake Law Review* 56 (2008), p. 958.

28. Foner, *The Second Founding*, p. 84.

29. Foner, *The Second Founding*, p. 84.

30. *Trump v. Anderson*, 601 U.S. 100, 144 S. Ct. 662 (2024).

31. The U.S. Supreme Court held that implementation of this provision requires congressional actions and states therefore could not unilaterally invoke it against a presidential candidate. *Trump v. Anderson*, 601 U.S. 100, 144 S. Ct. 662 (2024).

32. This provision has been tentatively invoked in debates about whether it is constitutional for Congress to refuse to raise the statutory debt ceiling to honor spending commitments already authorized through the biannual budget process. See Neil H. Buchanan and Michael C. Dorf, "How to Choose the Least Unconstitutional Option: Lessons for the President (and Others) from the Debt Ceiling Standoff," *Columbia Law Review* 112 (October 2012): 1175.

33. The Reconstruction Acts, 14 Stat. 428 (March 2, 1867), 15 Stat. 2 (March 23, 1867), 15 Stat. 14 (July 19, 1867), 15 Stat. 41 (March 11, 1868), 16 Stat. 59 (December 22, 1869).

34. Steven Levitsky and Daniel Ziblatt, *Tyranny of the Minority: Why American Democracy Reached the Breaking Point* (Crown, 2023), p. 76; United States Commission on Civil Rights, "Political Participation" (May 1968), pp. 1–2.

35. Foner, *The Second Founding*, pp. 52–53.

36. Foner, *The Second Founding*, pp. 98.

37. Kowal and Codrington, *The People's Constitution*, p. 112.

38. They also considered, but rejected, extending the rights protected by the Fifteenth Amendment to include the right to hold office without regard to race. Foner, *The Second Founding*, p. 104.

39. See generally Alexander Keyssar, *The Right to Vote: The Contested History of Democracy in the United States* (Basic Books, 2000), pp. 75–76.

40. Kowal and Codrington, *The People's Constitution*, p. 115; Keyssar, *The Right to Vote*, pp. 75–76.

41. Kowal and Codrington, *The People's Constitution*, pp. 113–115; Crum, "The Lawfulness of the Fifteenth Amendment," p. 1572.

42. Kowal and Codrington, *The People's Constitution*, pp. 113–115; Crum, "The Lawfulness of the Fifteenth Amendment," p. 1572.

43. Kowal and Codrington, *The People's Constitution*, p. 113–114.

44. Kowal and Codrington, *The People's Constitution*, pp. 113–115. See also generally Travis Crum, "The Unabridged Fifteenth Amendment," *Yale Law Journal* 133 (February 2023): 1039.

45. Travis Crum, "The Lawfulness of the Fifteenth Amendment," *Notre Dame Law Review* 97, no. 4 (April 2022): 1572.

46. Crum, "The Lawfulness of the Fifteenth Amendment," pp. 1574–1576.

47. Crum, "The Lawfulness of the Fifteenth Amendment," pp. 1572–1573.

48. Crum, "The Lawfulness of the Fifteenth Amendment," pp. 1577–1580.

49. Crum, "The Lawfulness of the Fifteenth Amendment," p. 1589.

50. Roosevelt, *The Nation That Never Was*, p. 96.

51. Foner, *Reconstruction*, p. 581; Allan Peskin, "Was There a Compromise of 1877?" *Journal of American History* 60, no. 1 (June 1973): 63; C. Vann Woodward, *Reunion and Reaction: The Compromise of 1877 and the End of Reconstruction* (Little, Brown, 1951).

52. Foner, *The Second Founding*, p. 146.

53. Foner, *The Second Founding*, p. 160; Akhil Reed Amar, *America's Constitution: A Biography* (Random House, 2005), p. 383.

54. Barbara Jordan (D-TX) and Andrew Young (D-GA) were elected to the House of Representatives in 1972. Paul Delaney, "Black Political Power Strengthened by 3 New House Victories," *New York Times*, November 8, 1972.

55. 83 U.S. 36 (1872).

56. *Slaughter-House Cases*, 83 U.S. 36, 66 (1872).

57. *Slaughter-House Cases*, 60.

58. *West Coast Hotel Co. v. Parrish*, 300 U.S. 379 (1937).

59. *Slaughter-House Cases*, 73–74.

60. *Slaughter-House Cases*, 80.

61. *Corfield v. Coryell*, 6 F. Cas. 546, 551 (Circuit Court of Pennsylvania, Eastern District, 1823).

62. *Slaughter-House Cases*, 75.

63. Decades later, "fundamental rights" would finally be brought under federal protection through the Fourteenth Amendment's Due Process Clause. See generally *Poe v. Ullman*, 367 U.S. 497 (1961).

64. *Civil Rights Cases*, 109 U.S. 3, 26 (1883).

65. Civil Rights Act of 1875 (or the Enforcement Act of 1875), 18 Stat. 335 (March 1, 1875).

66. See, for example, *Civil Rights Cases*, 41–43 (Justice Harlan, dissenting) (generally defining "public amusements").

67. *Jones v. Alfred H. Mayer Co.*, 392 U.S. 409, 439 (1968); see also Tsesis, "Interpreting the Thirteenth Amendment," pp. 1339–1341.

68. To see this clearly, compare the text of the Thirteenth and Fourteenth Amendments. The Thirteenth Amendment says simply that "neither slavery nor involuntary servitude . . . shall exist within the United States." The Fourteenth Amendment, in contrast, says "No state shall [violate the rights set out in the Amendment]."

69. Foner, *The Second Founding*, pp. 31–34.

70. *Civil Rights Cases*, 24.

71. *Civil Rights Cases*, 24–25.

72. *Civil Rights Cases*, 10; Foner, *The Second Founding*, pp. 140–142.

73. *Civil Rights Cases*, 24–25.

74. *Civil Rights Cases*, 24–25.

75. *Plessy v. Ferguson*, 163 U.S. 537 (1896).

76. *Brown v. Board of Education*, 347 U.S. 483 (1954).

77. *United States v. Cruikshank*, 92 U.S. 542 (1875).

78. Charles Lane, *The Day Freedom Died: The Colfax Massacre, the Supreme Court, and the Betrayal of Reconstruction* (Henry Holt, 2008), pp. 21–22.

79. Lane, *The Day Freedom Died*, pp. 21–22.

80. Lane, *The Day Freedom Died*, pp. 21–22, 265–266.

81. Lane, *The Day Freedom Died*, pp. 4, 203–204.

82. *United States v. Cruikshank*, 555–556.

83. *United States v. Cruikshank*, 556.

84. *United States v. Cruikshank*, 556–557.

85. *Giles v. Harris*, 189 U.S. 475 (1903).

86. *Giles v. Harris*, 482; Richard H. Pildes, "Democracy, Anti-Democracy, and the Canon," *Constitutional Commentary* 17 (2000): 299.

87. *Giles v. Harris*, 482.

88. *Giles v. Harris*, 482.
89. *Giles v. Harris*, 486.
90. *Giles v. Harris*, 486–487.
91. See generally Pildes, "Democracy, Anti-Democracy, and the Canon."
92. Foner, *The Second Founding*, pp. 129–131.
93. Civil Rights Act of 1964, 78 Stat. 241, Pub. L. 88–352 (July 2, 1964).
94. Upheld in *Heart of Atlanta Motel v. United States*, 379 U.S. 241 (1964).
95. Voting Rights Act of 1965, 79 Stat. 437, Pub. L. 89–110 (August 6, 1965).
96. Voting Rights Act of 1965, section 2.
97. Voting Rights Act of 1965, section 5.
98. Voting Rights Act of 1965, section 4; *South Carolina v. Katzenbach*, 383 U.S. 301, 310–12 (1966) (explaining the discriminatory use of tests and devices to deprive Black citizens of the right to vote in Alabama, Georgia, Louisiana, Mississippi, North Carolina, South Carolina, and Virginia).
99. Voting Rights Act of 1965, section 11(b), 3 and 12.
100. *South Carolina v. Katzenbach*, 323–326.
101. *South Carolina v. Katzenbach*, 325–327.
102. *South Carolina v Katzenbach*, 326 (citing *McCulloch v. Maryland*, 17 U.S. 316, 421 (1819)).
103. *South Carolina v. Katzenbach*, 328–330.
104. *Katzenbach v. Morgan*, 384 U.S. 641. 648 (1966).
105. Andrea Bernini, Giovanni Facchini, and Cecilia Testa, "Race, Representation, and Local Governments in the U.S. South: The Effect of the Voting Rights Act," *Journal of Political Economy* 131, no. 4 (April 2023).
106. John Lewis and Archie E. Allen, "Black Voter Registration Efforts in the South," *Notre Dame Lawyer* 48, no. 1 (1972): 114; Bernard Grofman, Lisa Handley, and Richard G. Niemi, *Minority Representation and the Quest for Voting Equality* (Cambridge University Press, 1992), pp. 21–22.
107. Grofman, Handley, and Niemi, *Minority Representation and the Quest for Voting Equality*, pp. 22–23.
108. Grofman, Handley, and Niemi, *Minority Representation and the Quest for Voting Equality*, p. 23.
109. Grofman, Handley, and Niemi, *Minority Representation and the Quest for Voting Equality*, p. 23.
110. Lewis and Allen, "Black Voter Registration Efforts in the South," pp. 114–115.
111. Lewis and Allen, "Black Voter Registration Efforts in the South," p. 126;

Grofman, Handley, and Niemi, *Minority Representation and the Quest for Voting Equality*, pp. 23–24. See also Travis Crum, "The Riddle of Race-Based Districting," *Columbia Law Review*, 124 (2024).

112. This is similar to the facts presented to the Supreme Court in an early Voting Rights Act case arising out of how city council districts were drawn in New Orleans. At the time of the dispute in that case, a majority of the voting-age population of New Orleans was African American, but no African American had ever been elected to the city council. *Beer v. United States*, 425 U.S. 130, 134–135 (1976).

113. 478 U.S. 30 (1986).

114. *Thornburg v. Gingles*, 478 U.S. 30, 34–35 (1986).

115. *Thornburg v. Gingles*, 38.

116. *Thornburg v. Gingles*, 46.

117. Voting Rights Act of 1965, section 2.

118. *Thornburg v. Gingles*, 50–51.

119. Pei-te Lien, Dianne M. Pinderhughes, Carol Hardy-Fata and Christine M. Sierra, "The Voting Rights Act and the Election of Nonwhite Officials," *Cambridge Core PS: Political Science and Politics* 40, no. 3 (July 10, 2007).

120. In *Regents of University of California v. Bakke*, only a single justice, Justice Lewis Powell, writing separately, posited that strict scrutiny applied to racial classifications that *benefited* rather than harmed racial minorities. 438 U.S. 265, 299 (1978). But by 1989, in *Richmond v. J.A. Croson Co.*, the use of strict scrutiny in such cases commanded a majority of the justices. 488 U.S. 469, 494 (1989).

121. *Shelby County v. Holder*, 570 U.S. 529 (2013).

122. *Shelby County v. Holder*, 536; *South Carolina v. Katzenbach*, 314.

123. *South Carolina v. Katzenbach*, 314.

124. *Shelby County v. Holder*, 537; *South Carolina v. Katzenbach*, 317.

125. *Shelby County v. Holder*, 537.

126. *Shelby County v. Holder*, 538.

127. Voting Rights Act of 1965, section 5.

128. *South Carolina v. Katzenbach*, 314–16.

129. *South Carolina v. Katzenbach*, 311, *Georgia v. United States*, 411 U.S. 526 (1973); *City of Rome v. United States*, 446 U.S. 156 (1980); *Lopez v. Monterey County*, 525 U.S. 266 (1999).

130. *Shelby County v. Holder*, 535–36.

131. *Shelby County v. Holder*, 553–54.

132. *Shelby County v. Holder*, 554.

133. *Arkansas State Conference of NAACP v. Arkansas Board of Apportionment*, 86 F.4th 1204 (8th Cir. 2023); *Alabama State Conf. of NAACP v. Alabama*, 949 F.3d 647, 662 (11th Cir. 2020) (Justice Branch, dissenting); *Robinson v. Ardoin*, 86 F.4th 574, 587–589 (responding to these arguments made by the state of Louisiana). See also Amandeep S. Grewal, "Discriminatory Intent Claims Under Section 2 of the Voting Rights Act," *Fordham Law Voting Rights and Democracy Forum* 2, no. 1 (October 2023): 25–28. *Allen v. Milligan*, 599 U.S. 1, 100 (2023) (Justice Thomas, dissenting); *Petteway v. Galveston County*, 86 F.4th 214, 218 (5th Cir. 2023) (vacated for rehearing en banc); Hayden Johnson, "Vote Denial and Defense: Reaffirming the Constitutionality of Section 2 of the Voting Rights Act," *Minnesota Journal of Law and Inequality* 39, no. 1 (February 2021).

134. *Mobile v. Bolden*, 446 U.S. 55 (1980).

135. Brief for Appellants, *Cooper v. Harris*, 581 U.S. 285 (2017), p. 26; Brief of Appellees, *Bethune-Hill v. Virginia State Board of Elections*, 580 U.S. 178 (2017), pp. 4–6, 35, 51; Johnson, "Vote Denial and Defense," pp. 89–105.

136. *Allen v. Milligan*, 599 U.S. 1 (2023).

137. *Allen v. Milligan* involved this type of issue. The question also has been raised more directly in a case pending at the time of this writing, *Louisiana v. Callais*.

138. *Adarand Constructors v. Pena*, 515 U.S. 200, 227 (1995) ("We hold today that all racial classifications, imposed by whatever federal, state, or local governmental actor, must be analyzed by a reviewing court under strict scrutiny. In other words, such classifications are constitutional only if they are narrowly tailored measures that further compelling governmental interests").

139. *Bethune-Hill v. Virginia State Board of Elections*, 580 U.S. 178, 193 (2017); see also *Bush v. Vera*, 517 U.S. 952, 977 (1996).

Chapter 6

1. William M. Van der Weyde, ed., *The Life and Works of Thomas Paine*, 10 vols., Patriots' Edition (Thomas Paine National Historical Association, 1925).

2. The full test is available at https://jimcrowmuseum.ferris.edu/question/2012/pdfs-docs/literacytest.pdf. It is worth grabbing a pencil and a timer and completing it without reading it first. Then ask someone else to grade it for you twice, once as if they want you to fail and then again as if they want you to pass.

3. Richard Hasen, *A Real Right to Vote* (Princeton University Press, 2024), pp. 70–72, 75–76.

4. Hasen, *A Real Right to Vote*, pp. 70–72, 75–76.

5. See *Brnovich v. Democratic National Committee*, 594 U.S. 647 (2021).

6. U.S. Constitution, Fourteenth Amendment, Section 1 ("No State shall make or enforce any law which shall abridge the privileges or immunities of citizens of the United States; nor shall any State deprive any person of life, liberty, or property, without due process of law; nor deny to any person within its jurisdiction the equal protection of the laws").

7. For a general introduction to equal protection analysis and tiers of review, see David S. Schwartz and Lori A. Ringhand, *Constitutional Law: A Context and Practices Casebook*, 3rd ed. (Carolina Academic Press, 2021), pp. 917–919.

8. Compare *Williamson v. Lee Optical, Inc.*, 348 U.S. 483 (1955), and *Brown v. Board of Education*, 347 U.S. 483 (1954).

9. *Harper v. Virginia State Board of Elections*, 383 U.S. 663 (1966).

10. *Bush v. Gore*, 531 U.S. 98 (2000).

11. *Crawford v. Marion County Election Board*, 553 U.S. 181 (2008).

12. *Harper*, 664 n. 1.

13. Michael Schudson, *The Good Citizen: A History of American Civic Life* (Simon & Schuster, 1998), p. 47.

14. Their use for this purpose was relatively short-lived. By 1824, as part of the broader democratization movement that swept the nation after independence, every state had embraced virtually universal suffrage for adult white men. Manisha Sinha, *The Rise and Fall of the Second American Republic: Reconstruction 1860–1920* (Norton, 2024), 43. See also "The Supreme Court 1965 Term: Poll Taxes," *Harvard Law Review* 80, 1 (November 1966): 176–180; Schudson, *The Good Citizen*, p. 182; Van Gosse, *The First Reconstruction: Black Politics in America from the Revolution to the Civil War* (University of North Carolina Press, 2021), p. 103.

15. Pro-enfranchisement critics of the Fifteenth Amendment objected to its text for exactly this reason. Eric Foner, *The Second Founding: How the Civil War and Reconstruction Remade the Constitution* (Norton, 2019), pp. 105-106.

16. Fergus M. Bordewich, *Klan War: Ulysses S. Grant and the Battle to Save Reconstruction* (Knopf, 2023), p. 107. See also "The Supreme Court 1965 Term: Poll Taxes" (citing "Notes and Legislation: Disenfranchisement by Means of the Poll Tax," *Harvard Law Review* 53, 4 (February 1940): 645–652) and John Kowal and Wilfred U. Codrington III, *The People's Constitution: 200 Years, 27 Amendments, and the Promise of a More Perfect Union* (New Press, 2021), p. 123.

17. *Yick Wo v. Hopkins*, 118 U.S. 356 (1886).

18. Kowal and Codrington, *The People's Constitution*, pp. 190–192.

19. *Harper*. See also Kowal and Codrington, *The People's Constitution*, p. 192.

20. Voting Rights Act, section 10; see also Bruce Ackerman and Jennifer Nou, "Canonizing the Civil Rights Revolution: The People and the Poll Tax," *Northwestern University Law Review* 103, 1 (Winter 2009): 63.

21. One might reasonably wonder if a poll tax imposed in Virginia in 1966 actually was nondiscriminatory, but the lower court in *Harper* had held that intentional racial discrimination was not proven on the record provided to the court. The Supreme Court accepted that finding and decided the case accordingly. *Harper v. Virginia State Board of Elections*, 383 U.S. 663, 683 n. 5 (Justice Harlan, dissenting).

22. *Yick Wo v. Hopkins.*

23. *Breedlove v. Suttles*, 302 U.S. 277 (1937).

24. *Lassiter v. Northampton County Bd. of Elections*, 360 U.S. 45, 52 (1959).

25. *Carrington v. Rash*, 380 U.S. 89 (1965).

26. *Harper*, 668.

27. *Harper*, 666.

28. *Harper*, 675 (Justice Black, dissenting).

29. *Harper*, 685 (Justice Harlan, dissenting).

30. *Bush v. Gore*, 100.

31. *Bush v. Gore*, 102.

32. *Bush v. Gore*, 102.

33. *Bush v. Gore*, 102.

34. *Bush v. Gore*, 147 (Justice Breyer, dissenting).

35. *Bush v. Gore*, 102.

36. The dissenting justices list more than twenty-five states using a similar standard. *Bush v. Gore*, 124 n. 2 (Justice Stevens, dissenting).

37. Presidential General Election Results by State, Federal Election Commission, accessed September 25, 2024, https://www.fec.gov/resources/cms-content/documents/FederalElections2000_PresidentialGeneralElectionResultsbyState.pdf.

38. *Bush v. Gore*, 105.

39. *Bush v. Gore*, 105–106.

40. *Bush v. Gore*, 105–106.

41. *Bush v. Gore*, 105–106.

42. See generally *Bush v. Gore.*

43. *Bush v. Gore.*

44. For a discussion of the relative novelty of *Bush v. Gore*, see Samuel Issacha-

roff, "Political Judgments," *University of Chicago Law Review* 68, 3 (Summer 2001): 648–650.

45. *Bush v. Gore*, 126 n. 4 (Justice Stevens, dissenting).

46. *Bush v. Gore*, 109.

47. See generally Ned Foley, "The Future of Bush v. Gore," *Ohio State Law Journal* 68, 4 (2007): 930–932.

48. Richard L. Hasen, "The Untimely Death of Bush v. Gore," *Stanford Law Review* 60, 1 (April 2010): 1.

49. Richard L. Hasen, *The Voting Wars: From Florida 2000 to the Next Election Meltdown* (Yale University Press, 2012).

50. Hasen, *A Real Right to Vote*, 102.

51. *Crawford*.

52. *Crawford*, 185–186.

53. Justice Breyer discusses many of these more permissive state laws in his *Crawford* dissent. *Crawford*, 237–241.

54. Bertrall L. Ross II and Douglas M. Spencer, "Passive Voter Suppression: Campaign Mobilization and the Effective Disfranchisement of the Poor," *Northwestern University Law Review* 114, 3 (2019): 642–643.

55. *Crawford*, 240 (Justice Breyer, dissenting).

56. *Crawford*, 239 (Justice Breyer, dissenting).

57. *Anderson v. Celebrezze*, 460 U.S. 780 (1983).

58. *Burdick v. Takushi*, 504 U.S. 428 (1992).

59. Justice Stevens describes the evolution of the *Anderson-Burdick* test in his *Crawford* opinion.

60. The Court split 3-3-3, which means there was no majority opinion. Justice Stevens's opinion reflected the outcome preferred by six of the justices, although those justices split on their reasoning.

61. The plurality opinion had to reach back to nineteenth-century anecdotes about New York City politics and the Tammany Hall machine to illustrate the risks avoided by the Indiana law. *Crawford*, 195 n. 11.

62. Justice David Souter discusses this in his *Crawford* dissent. *Crawford*, 227–228 (Justice Souter, dissenting).

63. *Crawford*, 196.

64. *Crawford*, 197.

65. Voter Confidence, MIT Election Data + Science Lab, accessed September 25, 2024, https://electionlab.mit.edu/research/voter-confidence.

66. *Crawford*, 199–203.

67. *Crawford*, 199–203.

68. *Crawford*, 201.

69. *Crawford*, 202.

70. See generally Hasen, *A Real Right to Vote*, p. 9.

71. Voting Laws Roundup: 2023 in Review, Brennan Center for Justice, accessed September 25, 2024, https://www.brennancenter.org/our-work/research -reports/voting-laws-roundup-2023-review.

72. Hasen, *A Real Right to Vote*, 106–109.

73. Hasen, *A Real Right to Vote*, 122–123.

74. Voting Laws Roundup: 2023 in Review, Brennan Center for Justice, accessed September 25, 2024, https://www.brennancenter.org/our-work/research -reports/voting-laws-roundup-2023-review.

75. Voting Laws Roundup: 2023 in Review, Brennan Center for Justice, accessed September 25, 2024, https://www.brennancenter.org/our-work/research -reports/voting-laws-roundup-2023-review.

76. See "Preserving and Protecting the Integrity of American Elections," Executive Order of March 25, 2025, https://www.whitehouse.gov/presidential-actions/ 2025/03/preserving-and-protecting-the-integrity-of-american-elections/.

77. Ross and Spencer, "Passive Voter Suppression," 642–643.

78. For an in-depth discussion of this issue, see Kevin Kruse and Julian Zelizer, eds., *Myth America* (Basic Books, 2022), p. 300.

79. Joshua A. Douglas, "The Right to Vote Under State Constitutions," *Vanderbilt University Law Review*, 67, 1 (January 2014): 89–90.

80. Douglas, "The Right to Vote Under State Constitutions," pp. 89–90.

81. Hasen, *A Real Right to Vote*.

82. Hasen, *A Real Right to Vote*, 153–155.

83. Hasen, *A Real Right to Vote*, 153–155.

84. *Yick Wo v. Hopkins*.

Conclusion

1. See, for example, Sanford Levinson and Jack Balkin, "Democracy and Dysfunction: An Exchange," *Indiana Law Review* 50 (2016): 281.

2. John F. Kowal and Wilfred U. Codrington III, *The People's Constitution: 200 Years, 27 Amendments, and the Promise of a More Perfect Union* (New Press, 2021), pp. 207–208.

3. James T. Kloppenberg, *Toward Democracy: The Struggle for Self-Rule in European and American Thought* (Oxford University Press, 2016), p. 344–345.

4. Keyssar, *The Right to Vote: The Contested History of Democracy in the United States* (Basic Books, 2000), pp. 140–141.

5. Keyssar, *The Right to Vote*, pp. 142–143; Kowal and Codrington, *The People's Constitution*, pp. 147–148.

6. Keyssar, *The Right to Vote*, p. 143.

7. Keyssar, *The Right to Vote*, p. 143–144.

8. *Minor v. Happersett*, 88 U.S. 162 (1874).

9. Keyssar, *The Right to Vote*, pp. 157–158.

10. Keyssar, *The Right to Vote*, p. 368.

11. Keyssar, *The Right to Vote*, pp. 174–175.

12. Kowal and Codrington, *The People's Constitution*, pp. 152–153. See also Keyssar, *The Right to Vote*, pp. 169–170.

13. Authenticated Report of the Ratification of the Nineteenth Amendment, Section 240, Women's Suffrage, U.S. Government Publishing Office, https://www.govinfo.gov/content/pkg/HMAN-104/pdf/HMAN-104-pg101.pdf.

14. Danielle Allen, *Our Declaration: A Reading of the Declaration of Independence in Defense of Equality* (Liveright, 2014), p. 268.

INDEX